CONFESSIONS OF AN INDIGO CHILD

An In-Depth Guide to Awakening Your Infinity

ALEXANDER PAPAGEORGHIOU

Confessions of an Indigo Child

An In-Depth Guide to Awakening Your Infinity

By Alexander Papageorghiou

ISBN: 9781795838856

Contents

Also available for your reading
and listening pleasure:

The Amazon link for the ebook:

https://www.amazon.com/Confessions-Indi-
go-Child-Depth-Awakening-ebook/dp/B07D5P-
1JM9

The audiobook link:

https://www.indigolightlove.com/books

I dedicate this book to my dear Oltida
for embodying love and compassion
in its purest form forevermore

Alexander

Preface

THERE COMES A time in everyone's life when they must commit to their destiny and choose the path that they know is right, even though the sound of their thoughts may get in the way. I always wondered how this book would begin, how one would compile the most inexplicably surprising path their life took on one sunny day, and the myriad experiences it placed in their way. This is the story of loss and pain, of rebirth and self-discovery, of a voyage to the soul, and getting in touch with ones' inner realm in ways mysterious to the conscious self. It is the story of the undeniable power of faith and hope, of the journey one must endure to know themselves, and of what life really means. It is living proof of the source of infinite love and knowledge that lies within us all, of the infinity that stands between us and yet binds us all together, this union of the tangible and metaphysical that creates the unique life form we call a human being.

I was asked, after years of journeying to the soul and rediscovering my true self in all its dimensions, to convey this experience through this book as a means of helping others in search of truth, by highlighting the milestones in their journey that may lead them in the right direction.

Self-discovery, in its essence, has a dual meaning. We always seek and discover, from the day of our birth to our passing. Yet, the Self is a term well effaced from common consciousness, as it begets not a journey to the boundaries of what the world has to offer, but a journey into what constitutes the spiritual being that makes us whole. Infinity is the correct way to describe the different paths to get there and the possibilities for interpretation. Truth is the vessel to get there, a truth that is self-evident and subjective, true only to the one seeking it. The universe relates to us as one of its particles. A similar universe of infinity lies within us, resonating with our particular frequency and consciousness. We are a universe in ourselves and to ourselves, each and every one of us. This is why it is so easy to relate to one another, yet often so difficult for others to comprehend us.

It is my belief that every living being on this plane and beyond is a spiritual one, searching only to return to the Source from whence it came. These words are meant to inspire the fact that all this begins within the heart of every single one of you, and that you must only look as far as yourself to encounter all the answers you ever sought.

We live in a modern world of contradictions, one where we attribute more value to what we own than what we are, and the more we pursue this, the further away we get from what we were meant to be. The essentials for your harmonious existence on this planet are already here in front of you, and ask that you acknowledge them so that you may live once again in touch with yourself.

It is an undeniable fact that the world is changing, that the planet is evolving, and that human beings feel now more than ever out of touch with their essence, as all the foundations around them are crumbling and there is nothing in sight to cling onto. The truth is that for solid foundations to be built the old ones must vanish, and in their rubble we are all reborn. Changing core values and human consciousness put the individual in the driver's seat, as this planet now depends on the cohesion and integration of all our energies. Subsequently, these depend on the cohesion and integrity of our own personal consciousness. Everything is cyclical and meshed into one another, and we are beginning to realize that. The power of global human consciousness is infinity in itself, but first one must find his or her own infinity. This is the story of my search for truth.

This is a voyage through time and space, through incarnations and streams of consciousness, a voyage through the spirit world, its guides, and our connection to Creation, the source of all-that-is. The last 4 years of my life have brought me to a point of rebirth. Most days I don't even recognize who I am or how clearly I can now see what I was blind to: the complexity of all planes of existence and truly understanding the notion of I AM.

I dedicate this book to all the seekers, the Indigo consciousness, my spirit guides and their physical counterparts, to the

Creator, and mostly to the infinity that lies before us as a race of human brothers and sisters. Thank you.

1.

Inception

SOME SAY ALL that exists in a physical state is actually the denser version of a thought-form and that life began in that way, as a complex spiritual existence on a different plane. We then descended into this state of being in order to experience and understand what it would mean to have limitations and conduct ourselves in a physical manner, witnessing all the tangible emotional states that may arise from this, like different synapses created in the brain as a response to various stimuli.

Life in a physical state does have its limitations, especially if you only live by them and are disconnected from their spiritual equivalent, disregarding the fact that what you deem a mere thought can become a physical reality. In such a manner, the further we stepped away from this ideology, the more we embraced emotions as a way of defining ourselves and surviving. This gave rise to the world as it stands today. What maybe arose as a thought-form called fear or anger, emotions we today deem as part of our daily routine, slowly crept in to overshadow the brightness that lies within us. What results is what you could leisurely watch on the daily news, while secretly fearing for your finances and ultimately for the dwindling commodity that is time, and what its erosion brings on your life.

As far back as I remember myself, fear and anger have been prized possessions in my cabinet, perhaps more than they should have been, becoming greater as the years passed. I was trying to find myself and the meaning of this journey that we call life. Things that seemed of the utmost importance to others, namely physical possessions, always seemed to me like a fleeting added-value to someone afraid they wouldn't add up if measured in terms of self-worth. Thinking in a manner that is out-of-the-box today can be bad for your health and securing a position in this world, whatever it may be. Yet, the strict definitions to which society desires you to adhere, and the niches it chooses for you, are not right for everyone. This has been the story of my life, a bane of sorts, until I learned how to turn it into a tool and use it to my advantage. Today, I understand the nature of this state of mind and the word it transcends that changed my life: INDIGO.

In the fall of 2007, I returned from an exodus in Spain to Israel, where I had grown up. By that point, my incarnation in this life had taken me from my birthplace of Switzerland to the Middle East, and then to my paternal homeland of Greece.

I was born into an upper middle class family as far back as I remember, one that always ensured there was plenty of all the necessary things, but a household that seemed to lack color and empathy from the very start. Childhood memories were vague for a long time, perhaps due to a selective mind which was not keen on remembering many things. The pattern that most marked me, stretching all the way to my mid-twenties, was the lack of cohesion within the family unit. This made it very hard, later on, to accept the notion of a nuclear family, a group of people ascribed to you by birth that you may or may not feel totally alien from. As far back as I can remember myself, I always lived in my own reality, making friendships difficult from childhood into adulthood. There is a transition that happens to most when they enter their teenage years: the selection of a group of belonging, which can mark their behavior and mold them in a certain way so that they are ready for life. These years also teach you to deal with the myriad emotions which you possess, which ones to bury and which to build walls around. This period, which can occur even in childhood, has a long-lasting effect on the survivalist behavior which later ensues. In a world of adversity and competition where love is a fleeting emotion, overburdened by physical responsibilities, a survivalist outlook is more profitable and long-lasting than vulnerability. You could call it emotional devolution. I found myself surfing through most of my childhood and teenage years afloat in my emotions, perhaps victimized by them, and no knowledge of self in order to address the reasons I felt the way I did. My surroundings always taught me that it was better to bury these, since our household was not able to deal with them. Things were thus buried or ignored.

The clearest thing I can remember was my sensitivity to everything, basically like a sponge, picking up on emotions, frustration, anger, and hidden notions between words, things people wouldn't want to say or to be known. This made things difficult throughout the years. People were hard to trust, and I had no way of putting my finger on what it was or how to control it. Only later in life, when I understood what it was meant for and how a spiritual outlook could help me, did I get this monkey off my back. Until then, I was overburdened with my emotions and others'. In times of conflict I could sit in a room and feel waves of electricity, like a physical manifestation of all the emotions that pervaded the room, beyond the silences and all things omitted. Often, that became unbearable and led to sadness or frustration, which then led to anger. These things have marked me as a human being since can I remember myself. Finding out that, later in life, this was not a curse and that I wasn't alone gave new meaning to everything.

This where the notion of **Indigo** enters. On the surface it is a word, a dark blue hue. Under the surface, it is a social message about things to come. I first came across it through my first spiritual teacher as she characterized my generation, a new wave of Old souls coming to this planet on their last round to make a change. After that, I surfed the World Wide Web extensively trying to get more information. I found very characteristic notions of what it meant to be part of this wave, almost as if people were trying to empirically characterize a new species of humans, and fit themselves within that mold, as they always strive to do. It said something about, from 1984 to 1996, souls incarnating on Earth that would be part of this energy and usher in a new age. They are rebellious and polemic, so as to change the ways of yore and distribute power and wealth equally in this ailing age. Adhering to strict definitions of things is what got us into the mess the world is in today, and only through introspection could we find who we are and where we are from. I do not desire to get into details about this wave as it has been covered amply throughout the media, alternative and mass. It is a symbol of things to come. It brings forth peace. It brings the promise of change, change from the old ways, the ones that got our planet and society into our current state of crisis. This word means everything to me as it gave me a sense of belonging, of social critical mass. I showed me that my generation was here for a purpose, to untie the knots of those who preceded us, to ensure that Gaia was saved from her demise, and that we could sustain life here in peace and harmony. This is the Indigo Consciousness, the key to our quantum leap in evolution. The day I found out I was Indigo was the day I could begin to decipher the enigma that was my life. Therefore, this is my story, through the eyes of an Indigo Child, as I perceive the world and the truths it has given me. It is all that I am today, all my faith, my love, and my compassion. I am a young man in my thirties like any other. I could be your son, your brother, your lover. Life has taken me on this journey, and I couldn't have imagined it would take such dimensions. These words are written in the hope that others find truth in this story, whether in themselves or those around them. It is a journey through the ages. In truth, it could be anyone's journey. That is the point, to find a deeper understanding of life and purpose in random messages we encounter in life. To find the journey to the soul we all yearn for, this would be the greater picture, but I did not know that yet.

The word only began to resonate with me when I read one of Lee Carroll's books and his accounts of different children that represented the different facets of this energy. One of them resonated so true with mine that, in that instant, I found out there were others in the same distress, searching for a higher truth that the physical world could no longer provide. He was greatly misdiagnosed as having a multitude of nervous disorders, committed to a psychiatric institution and never managed to find his path. It seemed his surroundings were adamant on classifying him as a textbook case of something with the tools they had at their disposition, rather than looking beyond all they knew for a greater understanding of things. This story of a marginalized youth, deeply sensitive and imbalanced, in an even more imbalanced world, brought me to tears. In many ways, all my life I had been him, medicated in order to deal with issues that were not addressable with the common means of modern psychiatry. The world is full of molds and Indigo children simply do not fit into any of them. They have incarnated here, many of them extremely old and knowledgeable souls, in order to break the molds of the status quo. The planet is evolving to a higher state of consciousness, and they are here to reform and tear down modern mindsets and their boundaries to make room for a new world.

This word resonated with me on many levels and helped me to understand that, even though I had mismanaged my emotions my life over and engaged in an everlasting search for a place within society, that search had been in vain because I already belonged to something greater than myself. This term clarified so many issues in my life, both physical and psychological, and gave me a head-start to begin deciphering what it meant to be me.

I later learned that the Indigo generation would bring mass change on the micro and the macro, only to pave the way for the Crystal Children who would teach the citizens of this planet a new way of living. These would be followed by the Rainbow Children, who would have Indigo parents, bringing about a new consciousness and evolution to this planet, both physically and spiritually, once firmly anchored in this new age. But I was to understand all this much later.

My teenage years were highlighted by many difficult moments, leading to an inner struggle greater than the battles we usually endure with ourselves in this formative part of our life. I sought to find an identity, a balance between sensitivity and strength, between the masculine and the feminine. Sadly, the male archetype often got the upper hand. One thing you must understand is that many Indigo children endure great ups and downs emotionally due partly to the magnetic polarity of their bodies. They physiques are meant to endure the changing nature of the Earth, both in terms of magnetic fields and an increased exposure to electricity and EM radiation from all the technology we are exposed to. If you add to that an increased sensitivity to the energies of people, and a sponge-like state of mind, it could be quite debasing to the balance of our bodies and mindsets, sometimes leading to eruptions of emotion and even violence. This perpetual "anger" and its propensity for physical outbursts, from sheer frustration, is something that haunted me for many years. The balance between the energies (masculine and feminine) was often upset. During the same time, my family life began to dissolve. Due to financial strife, my aunt took her own life when I was about 15, leading to a legal battle within the family that lasted for a decade. This brought forth a constant state of frustration within the house, like a field of electricity that might erupt at any time due to external stimuli. This charged atmosphere was very difficult for me to deal with over the years. I retreated into myself and found a sole outlet than marked me a long time: sedation. The indigo mindset is so sensitive and easily shifted that you can endure ups and downs almost instantaneously. When your emotions, such as anger or sadness, take hold of you, it is not proportional to the situation you are in, and you literally feel like you wished to die. It is a violent and extreme notion but increased sensitivity magnifies emotions to the point that they can get out of hand. This brings forth a new problem too common among Indigo Children that almost brought my life to an end more times than I care to remember: alcohol and drugs. They seem ominous to most, but to an overactive, malleable mind that seemingly never stops working, they are the only way to press the off button, albeit for a little while. They served me as an outlet until I had to choose between them and life. They marked my late teenage years heavily, and, along with medication for various nervous conditions, made functioning very difficult. Many experiences from this time that marked me are blurry at best. The pattern I do remember that took form during this time was a clash with authority and parents that prompted outbursts of pure rage. From an early age I suffered from a variety of disorders, characterized vaguely as ADHD, OCD, and so on. I was subjected to all sorts of medications and psychiatrists. These took part in my daily routine. Some would sedate me to the point of not being able to function, others less. My body would experience "electrical" charges that lead to outbursts of emotion. Today I manage these with meditation and conscious balancing of my energies. I could not read a single book until I was 25 from sheer lack of concentration. I was unable to sit and endure repetitive tasks at all, especially if they were trivial. As a young child I endured a debilitating form of math dyslexia referred to as Dyscalculia. I was totally incapable of deciphering the world of numbers and had trouble adding, subtracting, and such. This was to the point that I chose my college major because it did not have a mathematics requirement. I had no problem discussing complex, abstract subjects so long as I could visualize them, and I could memorize entire texts to the point of knowing where every indent and paragraph stood. I managed to finish my studies with the aid of speed reading and Cliff Notes, though how I graduated from high school still remains a mystery.

I had no idea how to deal with this physical and emotional load and neither did the adults around me, whether in the schooling system, or at home. They would ship me off to the designated therapist and medicate. I had to endure these trials and tribulations on a daily basis, with grown-ups basically standing as an obstacle, so stern and set in their ways, that they could not understand this as more than a cry for attention. Sadly, I was not alone. An entire generation was going through this at the same time. This new generation is meant to bring these foundations down. I often found myself confronted with the hypocrisy and blatant abuse of power of authority, whether in school or at home, and the hidden agendas that came along with them. This was something I could not tolerate to any degree. I believed for many years that I had a pathological disdain or distrust for authority, and could not fathom any person being "above" me in any manner. I always figured it came from a lack of self-belief. The clashes intensified until I was freed from the schooling system upon graduation, and could explore things on my own. From then my life slowly stabilized and I was able to put a debilitating marijuana addiction behind me, the scale of which is surprising to me even today.

The next few years were smooth in comparison to the past. I left for Greece to study, faced with new challenges, a new language and a country very foreign to me. It was a decision to go and explore a part of me that due to a certain family apathy was never revealed to me. I survived well despite some obstacles, whereby I had to break out of my shell to get what I wanted out of life. Greece taught me since the beginning that I had to be flexible for it since it would not reciprocate. I still believe that, up until the financial crisis that hit in the last couple of years, it was one of the more difficult places to survive. Sentiments towards Israel were not for the better and people were still wary of outsiders. Yet despite all that, I learned the language and by my second year was well social-ized. The recurring pattern was the metaphorical shedding of skin every 1.5 years, like if I found a new me and suddenly close friends vanished only to be replaced by new ones. This pattern, I noted, had followed me since very young, though it was not the uprooting or the international upbringing filled with nomadic diplomats that was the reason. I was to un-derstand this later. The main lesson I learned was confidence from the lowest and most survival-oriented point of view. If you are thrown into a society where you know nothing, you must surmount your insecurities and go out of your way to meet people and grow. Nobody will do it for you. I realized this soon enough and held it near to my heart since, despite having extended family in Greece, I had to do everything my-self. Only after maturing did I realize family isn't an inherent structure, but, like life in its forming, something you find along the way from the inside out. I would realize I had never been alone. Just because I couldn't see it, it didn't mean there weren't energies around supporting me and guiding me to-wards a new family.

With time, I finally and easily found my way. The ease and fluidity of it all gave me a lot of confidence, along with the feedback that I was capable beyond my comprehension.

This made me understand the necessity for the notion of **feedback**. The simple fact that we do not recognize or under-stand someone doesn't mean we shouldn't have the best and most positive message to relay to them. What parents and authority figures often deem to be constructive criticism can be detrimental to a youth's personality. Simply put, give the younger generation the benefit of the doubt, whether you understand them by your notion of truth or not. If you feel that you cannot do this in a certain capacity, then it is better to say nothing. That is all you can give them, and it is appreciation in its purest form, but I will elaborate on truths later.

My last year in college proved to be my biggest challenge. I was engaged in a destructive relationship and was forced to concentrate on my studies. My whole outlook began to change for the worst. The notable thing was the vanishing of people in my life as I fell into myself. I ended up facing the beginning of the hardest part of my life. I simultaneously lost most of the people around me and a very significant relationship, which would, in retrospect, be the great karmic element that began my spiritual awakening process. I managed to finish my studies with honors despite the bitterness in me over this period, and I left Greece, infuriated at my predicament. This was the beginning of my "Conscious Creation" process. Little did I know, at this stage, that my ever-decreasing state of emotions was attracting all the negativity which I was wary of, and I increasingly fell prey to my own fears, beginning a 3-year cycle of psychosomatic disorders. Yet, sometimes the best things come in the most ludicrous packages.

Upon finishing my studies, I left for Israel, very distraught, and settled back in the family home. This marked a new chapter in my life, albeit very disturbing, but also very constructive. I was faced with the reality of my family dynamic, another facet of my life that was being torn down in order to be rebuilt later. Studies do offer comfort since they are a mold where you remain for a good 4 years so that your life is spoken for. Once completed, you are to account for yourself, and are faced with the eternal question: what do you want to do with your life and what do you want it to mean? So, I began seeing the side of my family I had never wanted to see, in terms of their desires for my life versus what I wanted, what they deemed me to be and what I wanted to be. Furthermore, they decided to ignore my emotional state and the excessive drinking which followed. I firmly believe that we see who people are during times of duress, and only then can we understand what they mean to us. This was a process of very painful realizations for me, as I was left to deal with seas of pain that fell on deaf ears. The state I was in attracted more difficulties in the guise of health problems that were as well swept under the rug. I began to break at the seams. The confrontations at home were endless and, when I finally found employment in Spain, I left. This was all sweet and sour, an escape from a place that no longer represented a haven of any kind, that was no longer a safety net, to a place that I did not know. There is a time in everyone's life when they realize the illusion of the strength of family, and the sanctum withers away. We look at our parents age and lose their status as protectors in our lives. It is a stark realization of adulthood. It happens to everyone, perhaps sometimes in a smoother manner, but it is both terrifying, and after you survive it, empowering.

Beginning anew in Spain was the realization that you cannot run away from your problems, and that having my passport take me across the seas did not eradicate my pain. I was lost at work and the drinking and pain persisted, almost as if whatever state of emotions I was in became a physical reality almost instantly. I pondered upon this but disregarded it as nonsense. I had always been taught to bury my pain, so most people around me didn't know of the alcoholism and the depression. With time and insomnia, my situation got worse until I stopped working and fell into myself, getting ill and spending all day drunk and under the covers. By that time, I no longer spoke to my family. Next came the most marking experience in my life. It was the 29th of August, 3 weeks after my 24th birthday. I had been staying in some god-forsaken hotel costing me out of the nose and was drinking myself into an early grave. Every day was a copy of the one before like Groundhog Day, and I came to the realization, in one of my drunken stupors, amidst the pain, the anger, the illness, and the loneliness, that I could no longer continue.

I am not, nor have I ever been a religious person in any capacity. I have always been a skeptic but also somewhat gnostic. Despite my ultimate downfall, I was always guided by an inner sensation of hope. Even the faintest flicker is enough to ignite a new pathway and that was what I was functioning on now, my raison d'etre, because in our darkest hour sometimes all we have is faith. We do not know what it is or what it means but it is inexplicably there. By now, with insomnia induced depression and medical problems no one could cure, one should have given up because the physical world alone had no answer, and yet I had persisted. Since the age of 14 I had been under the guidance of a family friend, whom I will refer to as Y. She is an advanced Jungian psychologist and astrologer though she coins herself an existential counselor. Throughout all of my darkest times, she had been the voice of reason, using both psychology and astrology as tools to guide me. Since I had returned from Greece, I dwelled in astrology almost obsessively in order to get answers about myself and the future. In regards to the affirmation of Self and understanding my inner strength, it had been a very effective instrument even if many predictions were incorrect. It did bring forth a certain notion of unknown energies at work, and made me reiterate the eternal question: if we have this wonderful, mystical tool that can look into us, past, present, and future, it is evident that it was not man-made, so by whom or by what? That propagated this speck of hope that guided me. Many times I relied almost entirely on this, and yet it was not able to help. Regardless, I believed that I could decipher a way that would yield answers, since it was so adept at explaining to me what my strengths and weaknesses were, and where they originated.

Despite all that, I had reached the end of my rope and decided I would end my life. Now, this is a very conscious choice though it may seem erratic and careless. I would like to clarify a very distinct fact. We are born and given endless gifts in so many ways, most are things we do not even notice or understand. In the name of all the experiences, past, present, and future, that we face, for better or worse, and in the name of all the emotions that we have experienced, as well as the notion of what the ramifications of death and what lies beyond are…it is the most rational, cold-blooded, and utterly terrifying decision you can make. I had reached such a state of loneliness, like an abyss had been dug into my heart, and I was falling into it. After sending a message to my sister that I hoped to see my family in the afterlife, and that my passing would teach them to look through another's eyes, I proceeded to take all my sleeping pills combined with alcohol.

Such a decision is, funnily enough, much better made under the influence of alcohol or drugs. I am speaking of this for the first time since I promised this would be a confession book, and I am sure many young souls out there have made the same decision. I cannot think of anything more terrifying. The conscious choice that you have fallen so low that you are willing to leave everything behind and face the great unknown even brings forth all sorts of religious notions of the afterlife. I will never be able to fully describe this feeling. It is the deepest emotion of loss one could feel, losing oneself.

Despite this terrible outcome, I suppose I wasn't meant to go anywhere since I am still here, I don't know how I came out of this, fast enough to be rushed to the ER and recover swiftly. I kept it with me for very long and withstood the challenges that followed, empowered by the fact that I had survived this on my own, and so I was able to face another day. This downward spiral continued until I got severely ill and ultimately decided to leave and seek medical attention. I left almost overnight, filled with despair, back to Israel. My family was well aware of all I had been through but did not see me until many months later. In this moment of truth, I saw myself finally anchored in my own survival, and destined to run this out alone.

I eventually settled back into a daily routine while dealing with all my issues, and tried to create the semblance of a life with an emphasis on my career, convinced that some success would invigorate me and give me new momentum. Since creativity had never lacked with me, I came up with some ideas and put them into motion, but I kept on searching for myself in everything that I did. Over the next year and a half I engaged in many things, all falling apart due to lack of commitment or wrong timing, forcing me to reinvent myself constantly. I made some new friendships and was socially active, but the drinking had continued and drugs were now back into play. I alternated between periods of relative stability and endless, open-ended moves to try and progress. My physical and emotional problems persisted. My family was still distant. As always, people came and went. The constant that kept me going and drove me to seek more truth was my new-found appreciation for an inner strength I had seldom encountered. In retrospect, I could appreciate my ability to survive, and I believed that I could somehow prevail. Yet, in the long run, my problems were still there. Ultimately, as in the past, I was "creating" the negative world around me, attracting all the wrong elements out of my fears, and periods of soundness were followed by drug and alcohol-induced downfalls. The cycle was endless. An unfortunate mindset I had gotten myself into was that I could survive and find my peace in financial success, as if to "buy" my serenity. I would come very close to large and fruitful deals, only to be let down by potential business associates. In retrospect, most of these dealings, as they were rooted in fear and ego, were unsuccessful regardless. My failure to succeed actually salvaged me from ruin on a few occasions, after I had removed myself from these. I would like to get to the last and penultimate downfall which made me the person I am today.

For many months, I had been working on a certain endeavour with a cousin and his partner, promising great returns and abundant earning for us all in a very short time. The specifics are not important, but I must emphasize how reliant I was on this succeeding. I sincerely believed it would work and that the financial gain would be my salvation. I almost bought a house in this frame of mind. This entire project fell apart in May of 2009. I found out that my cousin and his partner had been misleading me about the promise of this deal for over 2 months, and that it would not go through. Considering all the investment I put into this and how much I counted on it, I was finally broken. Since it was the night of Independence Day, I did what I did best to relieve such problems. I made the conscious decision that I would drink myself into an early grave and that whatever would happen would happen. And it did.

After sunrise, I opened my eyes in a drunken stupor. I was lying in a ditch somewhere, my shirt torn off and my teeth shattered. It took me an eternity to pull myself out of this situation, and I finally arose and started screaming for help. I eventually realized that part of my face was cut open and that I had lacerations all over my neck and back. While chewing on remnants of my teeth, I screamed and no one came. In time, I found my way to the house where the festivities had been and an ambulance whisked me off to the hospital, only to find out I had been stabbed and my face cut open for some indiscretion the night before.

Now, all the gory details may seem like the lowest point and they probably were, but I will mark this as the greatest day of my life. I wandered through the hospital waiting room for 2 hours until I was treated, laughing, sedated and drunk, with the crystal-clear realization that this was the end. This was the end of my self-destructive behavior, the end of the end of this nihilistic attitude. I had to make a very distinct and affirmative choice, since another episode like this would probably be my last. That is the day I was saved from my own fear and detrimental behavior. I was laughing while looking up at the skies, understanding that sometimes, in the strangest ways, we are given a second chance. I vowed that this would be Round 2 of this existence. This time I was going to figure out what this was all about, this game we call life. I would uncover the nature of my despair, my pain, my hope, and my faith. I knew there was something greater than all of us that united us. I did not know what or why. I had tried a godless frame of mind for some time in the past, but that had lasted for a very short time. I quickly realized that if we were indeed just physical vessels in a purely third-dimensional reality, hampered by endless limitations, there was no salvation for me or the wreck that I was becoming. So began the story of my new life, and my rebirth into an entirely new sentient being, intelligent, compassionate, faithful, and connected from within. For that, I want to thank my guides, my angels, and the Creator, All-That-Is, for the eternal vigilance and guidance in my darkest hour, shining its brightest light and leading me on a path to self-renewal and discovery. All this happened because of one thing, one energy, one sentiment: **LOVE.**

2.

Rebirth

I HAD MADE A very simple, yet meaningful, choice in terms of its consequences. This asked of me to make immediate changes to my daily modus vivendi: releasing acquaintances that were no longer right, ending the endless, pointless debauchery that was my life at night, and most of all, leaving the alcohol and drugs behind. The most effective way to do this was to lock myself inside my house. It seemed simple enough, and it was. As soon as I found a purpose, a drive, I was set on a path with no coming back. I concluded that this incident was meant to teach me something very important and that this was a sign, not a random occurrence in the dark. How many second chances do you get? I realized I wanted to know what the world was really about beyond the physical realm we exist in every day, and what existing really meant. We exist in terms of our physical bodies, but in what capacity do we live? We grow up, study, work, copulate, procreate, eat, sleep, and grow old. Sometimes, and only sometimes, do we learn some lessons along the way. Most of us do not. We make whatever alterations to our lives, mostly those that suit us, but are afraid to tackle the greater existential enigmas the world holds for us. We all have our pondering moments, when we reflect on specific situations and their relevance to us beyond coincidence, but all is ultimately left unanswered. Because the world at large does not cater to these questions, they must come from a different place: within. This begins with a real and unequivocal desire to know all-that-is, and eventually to accept what it has to give us even if it is something we cannot explain. Since childhood I asked such questions. Often it was at night, speaking to the image of God, up high where I believed he was listening, telling him I was willing to go back wherever I came from. All he had to reciprocate with was an answer to any of the myriad questions I had asked. It turns out that we don't have to sacrifice or give up anything, since the answers are all here. We just have to listen, to tune into the frequency, like a radio between stations. It is simpler than we think since we do it most of our lives, especially during sleep. We call it intuition. I call it channeling your inner self. I will elaborate on this later.

One of the greater spiritual lessons is that there is no **coincidence**. This I would later learn to be true in so many ways. I found my path at home, alone, healing from my physical and emotional wounds, surprisingly not angry or looking for retribution from whoever was responsible for my injuries. I understood it was my doing. Many clear thoughts like this ensued. I strongly believe that only when we are faced with ourselves, can we listen to what we really have to say. There is no longer any place to run away to, like work, outings, or socialization. There is just us and the mirror. I do not honestly believe that, had I been in a serious relationship, with children, or even a demanding career, I could have understood any of the things that have led me to write this book. There is simply so much noise in this world, physical, energetic, and beyond, that we need the vacuum of our solace to tune in, and to face the personas and facets of ourselves that we leave in the dark during the rest of our lives. These are the deceitful, the insecure, the frightened, the lonely, the empty, and all the little children that we do not understand, that live within us. Because we never sought maturity, they never matured either.

There was one gateway which I thought I would try while researching spirituality: the internet. I believe the concept of a world that exists beyond our physical reality, that is ever-expanding and gathers endless accessible information, is a great metaphor for the Matrix beyond the 3rd-dimensional reality. My spiritual guides emphasized that this is precisely why it was created. As we now admit that we live in a global village, we are confronted with the notion of connectivity, and the endless opportunity for voicing ourselves through this medium. It does not attribute any importance to race, creed, color, age, or appearance. We are all inherently connected now in the physical world as in the spirit world. This virtual technological world mirrors the matrix that is our universal consciousness. This is an amazing feat, but it takes reflection to understand this side of it, beyond the emails and the Facebooking. It is safe to say that the internet served me well.

I started on the 2012 enigma, with all the different ideas about what it meant. It took me quite a while, researching and exploring all sorts of different subjects, relevant and irrelevant. I believe that the first thing that I would relate to was a YouTube video by Gregg Bradden. I cannot recall which one. It led me to other sources and similar authors. There were outlandish things, as I saw them at that time, about types of ETs and conspiracy theories, which I was not so much interested in, though maybe slightly intrigued by. I was basically poking in the dark, trying to find meaning, but I went by intuition. Little did I know that the reality we live in, along with its spiritual counterpart, are actually the equivalent of a totally outlandish C class movie, with their sheer eclectic nature and unfathomable experiences that lie in the metaphysical. Well, expect the unexpected, so don't expect anything. There were texts of stargates and so on, but I was captured by Graham Hancock and Gregg Bradden. I found my way to my Visa and must have bought close to 70 books within 2 months. I made it a point to sleep and then read all day, explore as my only daily activity until I found something. Information about the Matrix we live in, by Bradden, so well researched and tangible, captivated me. He talked about the use of the mind and the spirit to heal any ill of the physical body in his book "The Biology of Belief, " which related to the aforementioned brindle of hope I had in me this whole time. This was the faith of which I knew nothing, the understanding that there were miracles and inexplicable things even to the most advanced scientific minds. Graham Hancock talked of clinical studies with DMT, a chemical found exclusively in the pineal gland, the third eye as it is known colloquially. When administered intravenously in sufficient amounts, it took test subjects to other planes of existence, and recorded interactions with sentient beings that relayed information. I could easily relate to educated, researched points of view. Having studied history, political science and international relations in college, I knew how to spot a sensible writer, but I was not stopping there. I explored endlessly, through such bright minds as Steven Greer, Nikola Tesla, and so on. I was basically absorbing information and sleeping. This lasted for about 4 months. I was even, and I say this with a shameful smile, irked by Alistair Crowley, and treatises on Magic from Medieval esoteric texts, all very cryptic. When you are this hungry for knowledge and poking in the dark, you are extremely impressionable and sensitive to everything. You are solely guided by your intuition to separate the beneficial and the futile. Meanwhile, I was a regular on the internet, through the Project Camelot Portal and such websites, looking for answers. I was still also heavily involved with astrology, which became an even bigger obsession and was my salvation in this case. I had been researching it, trying to find its most esoteric roots, and had been reading on the Pauline Arts, basically how to contact the light beings we call angels, their nature, and their relationship to astrology. I found this fascinating and read on, even though the angelic kingdom was probably the topic I could relate to the least. Eschatological studies meant religion for me, and that had always been something I refused to adhere to, since I found it very counter-intuitive and illogical. I never infringed on other people's right to believe, and I can safely say that merely looking at the full moon on a clear night, it was difficult for me to doubt the existence of God.

He was definitely there, but frustratingly not tangible, and religion seemed to me as distancing men and women into a doctrine of black and white, right and wrong. These strict "moral" codes seemed to limit freedom, self-expression, and self-affirmation. I had refused to take part in this since my early childhood. Then there was the interest in history from my high school years, that turned into a college major, which made sure to propagate the idea that religion is so holy that it has divided the world and created so much hatred and utter prejudice. I mean, yes there are heavenly doctrines that are infused into our reality, but doesn't doctrine limit us and give the word of the ultimate Creator to select men, not women (for the most part), putting all our faith in their own personal doctrine, agendas, and human flaws? Messages do get skewed the more they are passed on, and everyone leaves a piece of themselves and their convictions in them, until they have lost their true form. As much as I didn't, and still don't, care for it, the only religion I do support is Freedom and Love. This requires all the compassion and tolerance we can muster, as hard as it is, since our truth is ultimately only relevant to us and our reality, not beyond.

We live in such a disillusioned and disparate world where everyone holds their truth to be self-evident, and have no shame about proselytizing in the micro and the macro. Truth is something I will elaborate on extensively later. It is something I have had to learn through my own need for tolerance, even towards those who do not tolerate.

I pursued my sudden interest in the angelic kingdom from

an esoteric perspective to see what it yielded. I believe it was mid-July by then. I was reading about the Sun and its ruler Leo, the sign I was born under. It elaborated that the Angelic rulership was of the Archangel Michael. I· was intrigued by that. I just want to note that the Creator and all its extensions do not have specific areas or times when they are more active or influential, so as to create the notion that Archangels and angels belong to certain days or signs. They are the manifestations of the Creator in all their beauty and are always there, equally invested in humanity and other races wherever they are. There is no nepotism, or preferential treatment in the light, only the choice to be part of the light or not.

That night I said to myself: "Okay, so I suppose I need a teacher that could bring me to the next stage of awareness, give me the knowledge of Healing, the esoteric, my soul, my Karma and how to tap into my channeling powers," by that time, the notion of channeling was no longer foreign to me, "so I ask you Archangel Michael, wherever you are, if you really are out there, to send me someone, somehow. Please, I would appreciate it forever." And so, I released this message into the unknown, flustered as to whether it would ever be answered. The following events are the beginning of my existence in a new state of awareness. They mark the threshold of a life beyond the physical, where miracles and the unthinkable are everyday occurrences.

Days went by almost in an instant. I found myself with the approaching date of my 26th birthday on my doorstep. The days leading to this had been rather uneventful and my exploration of the spiritual world had slightly stalled. I was simultaneously exploring the world of healing through meditation, working on certain areas of the body and using white light spells on my surroundings, not really understanding their true nature. I had been very inspired by what I had read on the inherent power of thought, and spent many nights actively meditating, trying to create my physical reality as I saw fit. I was sending energies of light to situations which I deemed dire, and trying to alter the moment. I have to admit some of it was working. I had just found a new apartment in which I would happily settle for 2 years, one that would finally serve as a beacon of peace, and enable me to begin a more concentrated and in-depth search for the truth I so longed for. I had a specific interest in frequencies and their power of activating sections of the brain, and I spent much time with Tibetan bowl and Schumann Resonance frequencies resounding through my ear canal. They apparently were attributed to specific mind-sets, such as compassion or intuition, and reverberated through one ear, binaural in nature, letting the brain compensate with a similar wave from the other ear, basically letting both sides of the brain join together in symphony. The right side, representing the feminine side and more in touch with intuition, is ultimately the link to the spirit world. The left is the one we use in logic-based, pragmatic decisions on a daily basis. It is safe to say that any process of spiritual awakening requires the activation and cooperation of both sides, synergy equaling harmony and balance. I let myself be absorbed by the physical and emotional process many nights over, opening a door to conscious active meditation, a practice which has probably saved and enhanced my life in ways beyond description. I would later learn about the impact of a single thought, positive or negative, on the physical realm. Sadly, as we are mostly consumed with worries and negativity, we bring these thought-forms into actualization in our physical world, without even the faintest idea how to cancel and replace them with positive messages. The main motif I understood from all the things I was exploring was the notion of the UNIVERSE. This was not the one described by astronomers and physicists, but rather a sentient consciousness that interacts with us on all the bases of our existence. It loves and cherishes us, and works as a tool for creation. The only downside, albeit significant, is its propensity for equating what we put out with the same response. If we, so to speak, feed it only negativity and fear as the wave of emotions that we emit, it returns all this in kind. This is a sort of balance, whereby you are the creator of your immediate and relative reality down to every single detail, no matter how insignificant. Unfortunately, a sheer lack of awareness of this power is detrimental to the balance we strive for in our lives, and this new age that is upon us. It is really asking for us to awaken and be conscious of this. This concept placed much emphasis on me as the mediator between different energies in my daily life, and made me feel positive and empowered about things to come.

The day of my 26th birthday had arrived, and after a rough and short night of eventful dreams, I awoke very early in the morning, definitely not something usual for me. I had been having the recurrent lucid dream, in my half-asleep state, of the Wailing Wall in Jerusalem, but I did not pay any attention to it. As I woke up and entertained a very early and welcome cup of coffee, it continued. It was probably around 8 by now and I decided that since this was a celebration, and I had not been to Jerusalem in almost 10 years, that it wouldn't be a bad idea to get on the train and head up there from Tel-Aviv. I decided to get dressed promptly to catch the 10 o'clock train, so as to not have the chance to change my mind and be conquered by my usual complacency. I was out the door promptly, arriving at the station and boarding the train. Despite being exhausted I felt somewhat elated. The sun was shining, and I was going on a short journey into the unknown, knowing that Jerusalem always holds surprises. Many more would come later on. I must have passed a few compartments looking for a place to sit, until I found a seemingly perfect spot where I was alone. I sat down, plugged my earphones into my iPod, and embarked on an early morning rock'n'roll journey. I was dozing off, somewhat, eyes closing and opening, alternating between states of consciousness. Soon enough, I opened my eyes briefly to notice someone sitting exactly in front of me. It was an elderly woman, probably in her late 50s, with a cherubic face and sparkling blue eyes. She smiled. She was dressed all in white, head to toe, with an indigo shawl around her neck. I dozed off again to regain consciousness a couple of minutes later. There was a piece of paper across the table. She had closed her eyes. They seemed to be rolling back into their sockets. She lifted her hand up and placed it vertically along the middle of her shoulders, like the little Buddha statues I had in my home. I was a bit flustered, wondering how someone doing this in public would be perceived. Little did

I know I would be a regular at this soon enough. She took a pen in her left hand, if I remember correctly, and began writing across the piece of paper. It was not the most correct thing of me to peek over to see what the letters were spelling, but I was compelled. She marked the date. The next words, in Hebrew, spelled "Dear Archangel Michael." I believe that second, despite how tired I was, a great shiver ran down my spine and my entire body, and my eyes began watering in a sort of ecstatic manner. The truth is I knew exactly what she was doing. I had been introduced to channeling through my reading. It had been 2 weeks since I had relayed to Archangel Michael, if he existed somewhere, somehow, my request. This was the day of my 26th birthday, suddenly compelled to go to the religious epicenter of the planet and encountering a woman, angelic in her own way, sitting across me, summoning the same being I had. It was too much, and even a skeptic like me, always searching for reason and logic, was dumbfounded. She kept on writing, but by then it made no difference what she wrote. I gathered the strength to ask her if she was channeling. She said yes, and cracked a large smile. I proceeded to tell her my story and she replied a simple "Well, there are no coincidences." I asked her if she had a card with her details. She promptly handed me one. I will refer to her as A. It read that she was a channeler, Reiki master, an expert in healing and in regression therapy. She told me she had a center in Tel-Aviv, not far from where I lived. I told her that I had been looking for a teacher that could ultimately combine all the disciplines I wished to learn. She told me that she had left the rural town of Kfar Saba to come to the city and open a center for the Indigo children, to educate them and help them find themselves. I was elated with all this. It was clearly the greatest present I had gotten so far. We kept on talking about other more personal things, and before I knew it the train had arrived in Jerusalem. I thanked her for her time and told her that I would come to see her. We both went our separate ways. I spent the rest of the day exploring Jerusalem's old city, even the family house where my aunt had taken her own life a good eleven years prior. I believe it served as a kind of closure as I began a new chapter. I was utterly exhausted by then but kept on walking on, reflecting on the events of the morning, and with doubt and my skepticism kicking in, I still wondered if this was for real, or if it was a coincidence or random occurrence. That feeling stayed with me for many months in all honesty. I learned later that "we have to believe to see, not to see to believe," and sometimes blind faith is necessary to begin having more physical and essential feedback from the Universe, as per the nature of our spiritual experiences. We cannot always get the answers or the messages how we want them to be. When they come, we must accept all that is, and release criticism and frustration. When we have surpassed all these obstacles and separated ourselves from our egos, these things reflect in our physical reality more and more. Even today, they still surprise me and ensure that they manifest only when I least expect them.

I passed through the Wailing Wall, always a spiritual experience that I believe surpasses the idea of religion. The place in itself is an energetic portal for our planet, a chakra for Gaia, our Mother Earth. Along with many others spread all over the world, the main one being in the Himalayas, these are a source of etheric energy for so many people. I would later, after I had finished my studies in A's center, be assigned a great mission at the Wailing Wall. This would make it for me, although I do not see myself as belonging to any denomination, a very significant place. I returned home that day exhausted and fulfilled, and I put the card on my dining room table.

It took about 2 weeks for me to pick up the phone and call the number on the card. I was anxious as to what might be, fearing somehow the unknown, but I knew I had to. Impromptu, one day I called. A young woman answered. Her name was Shlomit. She was gregarious, welcoming, and very positive. She invited me to come that afternoon to the center and get acquainted, and within hours I walked through that door. I never looked back. I cannot say that I was not weary and skeptical about the place, as when we do not know what to expect, we imagine things the way we wished they were. There I met Shlomit, eyes sparkling with kindness and honesty, and we sat down and talked for what was probably hours. She told me of her own pain and journey that had led her to the center, the change she had made in her own life, and her new-found love and appreciation for herself now that she knew what her life path had been trying to tell her. I was surprised how comfortable I felt, despite not knowing these surroundings. She emitted a certain warmth and non-judgmental attitude I had seldom encountered. That day I signed up for the first course I was to take, called Connection to the Soul. It enabled me to clean ancient spiritual wounds and karmas that we have harbored for so long, and that resonate into our physical reality on a daily basis. I was to learn the nature of the spiritual world and the path of the soul, as well as my own journey through the ages and incarnations back to birth, peeling off one layer at a time. As there are physical wounds that we keep with us through life and sometimes heal from, there is a spiritual equivalent when we experience a fall in our energies. This is when we can say we are hurt without physically being so. These wounds sit along the alignment of chakras and block the one they correspond to. As we accumulate these through the ages, they come back into our lives, sometimes bound by karma to other people, and we encounter the same scenarios incarnation after incarnation, until they are addressed and reconciled with. Imagine the myriad incarnations we have lived through, sometimes from before time even existed, and all this negative energy we have accumulated. Then, we wonder why we are blocked in many areas of our lives, why we get ill, and why patterns keep on repeating themselves throughout our lifetimes, all mirroring what we are meant to be dealing with. It is endless, and if not confronted at a certain time, it is no wonder we age so quickly, often succumbing to bitterness and cynicism.

The basic spiritual principle is that what is above is below. Every single thing that we encounter here in the now is a reflection of what is above. In the etheric realm things are not bound by time or physical limitations, hence they happen instantaneously, for better or worse. We can alter a life-long pattern with a single thought, and restart it a second later. It does take infinitely more time to come all the way down here into the 3rd dimension, the most physical of all states, where the more densely compacted energies exist. Yet, by the time they have reached here they are already manifested in the now. We ultimately pay the price for our negativity and indiscretions by way of thoughts without even knowing otherwise. The point of this course was to give me greater understanding of this, but I honestly had no idea of the magnitude it would take, or its ultimate influence on me.

Around the same period of time, I had moved to a new apartment and begun a venture in jewelry, opening a luxury items store on the internet. I had safely started a new chapter in my life and saw things bear fruit in this short time, more than ever before. This business would again be metaphoric for creating something physical from the vision which one had, and grounding an idea, a simple thought-form that existed before as random energy somewhere. The creative process was great fun. I always knew that I could not survive in an environment where I would serve another as a sort of corporate underpaid pawn. This was a realization I must have had from my early teens. The only way I could thrive was to create something of my own and be my own master, without the blockages and frustrations of a larger enterprise riding on my back. I believe we are all, in some capacity, meant to create, and that the modern corporate environment seeks only maximize your output and attribute a certain monetary value to you and your time. It ultimately prevents you from fully realizing your potential. This was not something I could fathom. I kept at my task, seeing this creation take form and become a reality, as I began a new chapter in my life.

3.

Ascension

A NEW ME WAS born as I stepped into this spiritual center for my first course, not knowing what to expect, and I began peeling off the layers. Slowly, through the first lessons, I got acquainted with the different physical and spiritual energies of the body: astral, electromagnetic, etc... We talked about the Higher Self and the extensions of the Soul, whereby it was originally created as a huge energetic entity that got fragmented into multiple particles which ended up in different bodies. This would be referred to as your soul group. As soon as someone entered an awakened state of being and began ascending through the stages of consciousness, he or she eventually became the main vessel for the soul, enabling them to identify almost entirely with the soul as their own. The ideas of karma, dharma, and nirvana were reiterated, but in more details than I had seen them before. To simplify, the idea was that the soul was always trying to reach balance, the one it began with, and to return to its ultimate state of being. Through certain behaviors in all of its incarnations, decisions were made that did not benefit the soul. It thus began the cycle of karma and was bound by it. It sought to return to dharma, the ultimate balance. Karma is essentially not the elements that bind you to people or situations from which you are meant to learn, but the specific set of experiences and events that are meant to awaken you so that you may solve and release said main karma, and achieve balance. There are a multitude of lesser karmas that bind us to almost everyone in our lives, past, present, and future, and these are secondary to the main one. Nirvana is the ultimate state of being, one where all is light, and we exist free of any karmic chains. Unfortunately, in our modern-day lives, we do not even reach this basic point, and have gone through the same lessons lifetime after lifetime, in order to achieve balance, yet mostly never getting close. This New Age is thought of as the last incarnation for many beings of light, one that encompasses all of their experiences and lessons from all prior lifetimes. What we are dealing with now is cumulatively resolving all of the issues we have repeatedly dealt with since our first incarnation separated us from the Source. As we approach the year 2012, we are entering, as predicted by many ancient civilizations, a New Age of Ascension, from the 3rd dimension/density state of being (physicality, struggle, and fear) through the 4th dimension (where time and karma exist, the beginning of physically intangible concepts and ideals), onto the plane of the 5th dimension, whereby we reach full awareness of ourselves and combine physical and spiritual. Time ceases to exist in its normal form and we are able to access all the levels of our Soul throughout the space-time continuum, past, present, and future as one fabric. We awaken to all our karmas and reconcile with them, starting a new chapter of awareness. The slate is blank and all of our being, physical and etheric, is infused with light down to the cellular level. We are able to consciously create our reality as we desire it, while aware of how our fears, ego, doubt, and criticism affect our decision-making.

During the course, I was able to retrace my story to the beginning of my existence as a spiritual being and work my way to the now, through all the incarnations and lessons I had learned. The point was to identify "spiritual wounds." Just as we can cut our own flesh and subsequently bleed, we are also susceptible to wounds of a non-physical nature that bring our energy down, even for an instant, and get stuck to our auric field and our spiritual body for as long as we do not resolve them. We can do so by addressing them directly, or by making life-changing decisions that would eradicate their root of the issue. If you compile all of these wounds up until the now, the burden is too much to bear for most. The purpose was to clean the etheric field, so that the physical vessel and reality may benefit. There are so many of these wounds that it is indeed impossible to address them all, but the major ones that mark our current lifetime, traceable throughout our myriad lives, are those that must be cleared. These are the tools we received in this first initiation to the practicality of the spiritual world. I was beginning to understand the link between the two, the instantaneous impact of my thoughts upon my physical reality, and how they affected my daily life. The change was that I was beginning to recognize these patterns and to map out the situations they had led me into in the past. As I worked my way progressively through each session, experiencing vivid visions of the past, I relished the fact that I finally had a framework in which to explore and thrive. I was surrounded by people like me, that wished to get to know themselves from the inside out. There were still many obstacles to face, the main one being my skepticism. At the beginning of such a journey, despite the teacher that was sent to me out of nowhere on a "random" day, most of these voyages occurred within the mind, where reality is split into so many different, subjective levels. You only have your intuition to guide you, as the physical plane does not provide you with feedback that corroborates your visions. This is ultimately a lesson in faith, sometimes blindly so. It is imperative in these situations where "reality" and "imagination" start to blend, at least from a conscious, rational point of view. Unfortunately, it took me many months to trust my own feelings, after I had learned to listen to the voice of truth that resounded from within. Some of these things seemed totally illogical and improbable, but all the fibers of my being resonated in one frequency, unanimous in their message that what I was feeling and thinking were now one, and that my experiences were as real as the chair I was sitting in. Around that time, I would often meditate late at night, accompanied by frequencies or Tibetan bowls sounds, entering into deep theta mind states, and experiencing very clear voyages through time and space, sometimes not knowing where I was, what form I was in, or if it was even my journey. I was endlessly exploring and sensing what it meant to travel into and through the mind. Modern science recognizes the brain as a collection of fatty tissue fueled by glucose, with neurons and synapses creating pathways of information, a very physical concept. The **mind** is something else, it is a beautiful and nebulous thing. I believe it is inherent that there is such a thing as consciousness, but the idea in itself is evasive at best, something that perhaps exists somewhere, sometime. More complex would be the link between the two, how the physical brain cooperates with its etheric counterpart. If you recognize the basic esoteric ideal that what is above is below, that every physical thing is a manifestation of a higher spiritual archetype, you can begin to see how this vessel could allow you to travel wherever you wished, even breaching the barriers of time. Locality is a very physical concept. You could, for example, be imprisoned in a tiny cell for a very long time, bound by the physical world to a very specific location. Yet, nothing in existence could prevent your consciousness and soul from leaving the body and exploring, travelling back and forth through the infinity of time, space, and all that lies beyond. This is something every human does innately while sleeping. It allows the body to regenerate through a state of inactivity, and the soul to leave the body and experience its own renewal by drawing on cosmic energies. It can also accomplish many tasks during that time. If you pay close attention during lucid dreaming, or even while asleep, by pausing and getting to know your surroundings and the situation you may be in, you soon realize that time itself is warped, minutes can give you the impression of hours or even days, or the opposite. Time is also, like locality, a physical concept highlighting the constant movement of the planets as they orbit each other, a linear measure of our lives as the body ages and withers away. This is a 4th dimensional idea, that we are bound on this path to somewhere. Yet, the mind transcends all of this and grants you an escape into infinity. The greatest challenge in the beginning of this new journey was the combining of Heaven and Earth, so to speak.

As I explored how the two were linked, focusing mainly on the Heaven part of the equation, I was having difficulty functioning on the physical plane. I believe that the day I met A and began studying at her center, was the affirmation I made that I was leaving my old life behind, and that my reality would never look the same again. It was as if someone revealed to you the essence of life on some occasion. You would probably spend the next months walking the streets of your city, aghast. You would have understood that the world was not at all what it seemed to be, that your life was very much like the Matrix, whereby the reality you were experiencing was really an incomplete, lesser part of the picture, and that what you knew to be true really wasn't. Your mind would be boggled by the sheer magnitude of what it meant regarding every aspect of your life. The illusion of your "reality" up until that point would have been shattered. This is basically what I was experiencing, though much less dramatic. I had contacted a being that existed only in certain textbooks, and next thing you know I was studying with one of his appointed masters in a context that was anything but ordinary, knowing that the impossible was to become a daily ritual for me. My routine after waking up and starting my day, despite having had mind-blowing experiences while meditating the night before, was often grueling. The pure physicality of it all, and the nature and behavior of people, were proving to be difficult. After having had the most perfect, balanced voyage within the infinity of consciousness, to go out into the heat of Middle-Eastern summer and brace all sorts of unsavory experiences throughout the day became more of a challenge. I knew that the lesson was ultimately as physical as it was spiritual, and to reach infinity, just like in the glyph, one had to embrace and unite both worlds, as he or she stood at the crossroads.

Meanwhile, I persisted on this journey towards my own light. With the removal of every single spiritual wound, I was brought me closer to my objective and I cherished all that I learned from it. I remember fondly one such experience. It was an awakening in itself since it stirred up emotions that I did not know existed. I was in Atlantis or Lemuria, two lands of the distant past that exist today only as fiction. There was an island slowly sinking into the sea. I watched the scene from below the blue hue of the surface as a whale. The background was filled with whale sounds, cries of suffering and discord. They permeated the waters' solace and I could hear the screams of humans in the distance, watching an entire civilization, and the souls bound to it, perish in the immensity of the sea. Bodies broke through the surface and floated lifelessly while I watched, completely helpless. I had encountered many visions of Atlantis, Lemuria, and other distant pasts before, but none as vivid as this, and so I began to cry. I muffled my tears as it was not something I was keen on doing, but they just kept on coming, as if I was empathizing immensely with these lost souls, all through a vision of the mind. It could have been a daydream for all I knew, but it wasn't. Emotion had to come from somewhere, have some legitimacy, a beginning, and an end. And so, I wept. I don't believe I have cried like this since. It awoke something in me, not of sadness, but rather of the reality of this new experience. I mean, how could one feel so much pain, such genuine emotion over something that wasn't "real"?

Despite this renewal of faith, skepticism still lived comfortably inside me, periodically dropping by for a visit. It was about the same time that I decided to take a short vacation to the Negev, the desert that lies in the south of Israel, adjacent to the Sinai. I wanted some distance between my daily life and myself, and some time to reflect upon all my lessons and what I had experienced in the last few months. This was around November 2009. The desert was still thriving, hot enough to dehydrate you in an instant, and quiet enough so that you could hear your own thoughts. To this day, I still do not think there is something as picturesque as a desert landscape. The emptiness, the quiet, it is a place where time stands still and does not lurk in to disturb you. It is by far the only place in Israel where you can walk for miles and not see a soul. A far-cry from the urban landscape of Tel-Aviv, it has the exotic feeling you would get from the Serengeti or the Sahara, but is only an hour and a half by train. I found some little cabins that offered me shelter and took with me as a companion "The Tibetan Book of Life and Death" by Sogyal Rinpoche. I moved to a second location which had no electricity, and finally understood the meaning of being with yourself. The quiet was intoxicating. I found myself to be more and more sensitive to my surroundings as time passed, able to hear, see, and smell much more than before. Often, it was difficult to live in the context of Tel-Aviv, a noisy Middle-Eastern city, constantly under construction, where the atmosphere is filled with an almost electric feeling of stress. Finally, I was as isolated as could be, in the middle of nowhere, where the only disturbance could come from me.

On one of the days, I decided to go on a short walk in a valley near my cabin. I did not take water with as I did not plan on going too far. I kept on walking and somehow could not stop myself. I think I had ventured way too far by that time and would still have to return. The thing about the desert is that, despite the scorching heat and the endless sea of sand, you can dehydrate without even knowing it until it is too late. I was approaching that state, and cursed my kamikaze notion of life. I was in the middle of nowhere and had to begin heading back, having had a tingle of fear that prompted me to realize this was not a game. I must admit that pushing boundaries has always been a source of excitement for me. I believe that most of my life I didn't really care for, or calculate, the consequences, and took all sorts of idiotic risks. It was a very do-or-die attitude. In the adrenaline lies the notion that you are ultimately careless for your existence and well-being, if you could throw everything away for a moment of excitement. I have put myself in harms' way more times than I care to remember, and I understand now that there has always been someone watching, making sure I made it to the day I could record this. The difference is that, when you have something to live for, you begin to calculate and take precautions.

When I affirmed that I wanted to stay here, and take another shot at life and what it had to give me, I realized it's fleeting nature, how fast it could end, and I started taking better care of myself in many respects. Unfortunately, this did not include random acts of stupidity masked as valor.

As I felt that tingle up my spine I asked for protection from my guidance were anything to happen to me, and I realized I was quite lost as well. I took a deep breath and kept on walking in the direction I felt was correct for me. A few minutes elapsed and I heard what seemed to be an engine in the background. The only problem was that I was literally in no man's land. There was no road, no path, nowhere to entertain a set of wheels. I turned around to see a man on an ATV approaching quickly towards me. I was stunned. He stopped right next to me and asked me what I was doing there. Before I could answer, he took out a huge jug of water and asked me to start drinking. He was a Bedouin, accustomed to the desert, but far from any settlement. He then told me to jump on the back of the vehicle and that he would drop me close to the cabin. I had a smile hiding in the corner of my mouth, as I knew this could literally be heaven-sent, but I preferred to still remain with a slight doubt. As I reached the cabin I thanked him in Arabic and bid him farewell. This would be one of many experiences that defy logic, that would across my path within the next 2 years. Eventually, I would learn to believe from the inside out, and trust that miracles do occur, on the micro and the macro. The next day, I went on another little excursion that went awry, though this time with water. I was stuck within valleys and had lost my direction, no compass or even cell phone at hand. I decided to climb onto one of the hills that were quite steep, for a vantage point. I realized that were I to fall and twist my ankle, get bitten by a rattlesnake, or not return before sundown, I would be in a world of trouble. I again asked for protection and a sign. I still could not find my way. As I reached the top, a large bird flew above me and as I followed with my eyes the direct line made by its flight, I found what was the vague outline of my cabin. Eventually, I made it safely back and promised myself I would avoid irresponsible desert missions in the future. Two days, later I was back in Tel-Aviv, reminiscing on the beauty of such a landscape. I was amazed, on the train ride home, at the sheer contrast of this tiny country, so many different facets on a simple one-and-a-half-hour ride. From the desert landscape with Bedouin settlements, throughout the entire spectrum of demographic and socio-economic levels within such a short time. Such wealth and such poverty juxtaposed, with the government none the wiser, a country so disparate and out of touch with its identity that you could get such a range of emotions and sceneries in 90 minutes. I also reflected on the book I had read, a Tibetan outlook on the nature of life and death, the continuous journey of the soul. I was pleased to see that it basically coincided with what I was learning, from understanding karmic baggage to how to deal with entities that exist in our etheric reality, what we basically refer to as ghosts. All these different lessons were compiled into a wise book, that reinforced even more the feeling that I was on the right path. I must have read more than 50-60 books in these months, most speed-reading until I had extracted what

I felt I needed from them. The consensus was that, on many levels, since I was learning from my own inner experience I could no longer benefit as much from outer sources. As soon as I could, I would learn how to access the pools of endless knowledge that lie within our universal consciousness. Later on, I would use books only as reference points, in order to direct my search in a specific direction with channeling and meditation.

As everything that is above is below, so is knowledge. No knowledge is new, only transcended from one place or plane to another, as nothing is an innovation, only a reiteration of something from some other place or time. All knowledge that we tap into exists like a cloud within the universal consciousness. We can access it at any time in multiple ways. We do so, for example, when we innovate. We basically pass on what we have learned from one place to another. So, the contents of books exist in the same manner, whether we see them as containing clouds of knowledge pertaining only to the writer, or whether they teach us more wholesome, universal lessons that originate from high above. Therefore, knowledge, though it has an actual form and substance like matter, is non-local, and exists everywhere and nowhere all at once, accessible through and from infinity at any given time. This is the true nature of the dimensions of the Universe. They exist and do not, simultaneously, at least by our human notion of existence. Can we fathom what existing in the 12ᵗʰ dimension would be like? What would it mean as per form and identity? It would shatter all those parameters and therefore only exists, at the moment, in theoretical quantum physics.

Like we can effortlessly bend the fabric of the space-time continuum with our consciousness, we can also do it on a more physical level, which will one day enable us to time travel. We must simply stop trying to rationalize by our standards what is real and what is not, and subsequently what is feasible and what isn't. I do not, under any circumstance, pretend to know the secrets of the Universe and the endless answers to the paradigms of time and space. Yet, I accept that I am a spiritual being in a physical vessel, that is not bound beyond my physicality by anything but my own fear, skepticism, and ignorance. I also do not need to understand the nature of all I am doing in order to do it. Consciousness is infinity and therefore infinite in capabilities. That is all I need to understand in order to venture into the future as a conscious being of unlimited potential. The same applies to every living being on this plane and beyond. Accept your infinity, your godliness, and become unlimited. The physical world is a mere reflection of the conscious and unconscious choices we make in our "mind's eye," where visualization can become reality. Whether we do this correctly and for our benefit, or we fill such a vision with fear and anger, is a choice. The differentiation lies within the awareness. The more we raise our awareness, the more we awaken our godliness, our ability to consciously and lovingly create, and we enter the Supreme Design stage of our lives. Ultimately, when I coin the phrase "godliness," I refer to the ultimate state in which we were all created and to which we have the ability to return in the 5th dimension, where thought and mind are reality.

The infinity we call God presents itself as the Creator. It is precisely that. We were made in its image and innately possess this trait, the ability to create. We must simply be aware enough to tap into that energy, so that we may apply it to our lives and mold it according to our truth and purpose. The aforementioned awareness depends on our decision to embrace a more spiritual life, whereby we establish a search to return to that root essence, that godliness. Following this, things slowly unveil before our eyes. All that we are is all that is. Nothing more, and nothing less. If you think about it, creating is the essence of our lives, the physical and spiritual connection to what we are as a species. Look at the world we live in, from reproduction to endless innovations in medicine, technology, as well as art and music. These are all byproducts of this essence that we call Creation. In conclusion, the gifts we inherently possess and see as secondary traits of our nature, more apparent in some than others, are an inherent part of our link to the infinite. In our smallest, most precise, and in our largest, most outlandish visions of creating, we find our godliness. The next time you come up with a great idea, crack a smile in the name of your infinite godliness, and maybe pursue it. If you peer into the eyes of your newborn, reflect not only on your entry into parenthood or in the miracle that is life, but in the ultimate Creation that came from you and your partner.

By this time, I was back home and to my studies, nearing the end of my first course. I was still experimenting during the dark of night with astral voyages and visions of a distant past. Parallel to learning, I also took part in personal sessions with my teacher to tap into myself and my abilities. I kept on getting great channelings from her that were defining my purpose on this planet at this time, as well as the reasons I had experienced all that had transpired in the last 4 years. I was building my confidence up for the first time, from a totally different place, not relying on appearance or materialism This was no longer a nebulous version of self-worth that could implode at any given time, but building foundations with a deeper understanding of love, and guidance from within. I was getting in touch with my guidance on the spiritual plane and they spoke to me through my mentor and others, helping me in this burgeoning stage of my spiritual evolution. The course ended with tracing our life back to birth in this incarnation. Birth, it seemed, was a great spiritual wound in itself, as it was a frightening physical process since we are programmed not to remember anything as we are reborn onto the physical plane, amplifying feelings of loneliness and disconnect from the Source. The significance of this journey lies in its transition through two very different existences, and the creation of a new vessel and face for the soul. I believe it is important, not because of the message I received during the session or the magnitude of a rebirth, but because of the sheer satisfaction of holding the infant version of me in my arms within my mind's eye, and conveying to this newborn the energy of confidence and safety that he would ultimately feel as he reached 26 years of age. The road would be very rocky and steep at times, nearly falling off the edge, but if he asked you if it was worth it, what would you answer? "Absolutely! You will understand everything in due time, the nature of life, and feel safe and sound in your budding adulthood. This is a promise. Just know that you are loved by forces greater than you know." Perhaps it mimicked the feeling of a father holding his child in his arms. I was marked by the sheer security I felt, after rising from the great unknown for so long, this silence and inner peace showing me that somehow, somewhere, everything would turn out for the best. Elation followed. "Little man, you will be fine, remember that," and I left him with this new energy as it was imprinted in him and spread throughout his future, until the now I was physically in. It would correct and change the path and wounds I had collected from this specific event throughout my lifetime. This is possible because time is non-local. Thus, the past, present, and future exist all at once, and even if the past is no more, its energy can still be altered in order to release parts of you that may affect your present and future. So, "let bygones be bygones" is fine, but even if they are gone they still are. The nature of time is so complex that I don't know if I will ever fully be able to grasp it.

All of this experience was ultimately a reflection on the long and hard journey I had gone through from birth to this point, and for the first time I knew some truths to be real in terms of their impact on my life. Truths are very subjective, but I don't honestly believe that we know anything until we really know it. This requires us to understand the Heaven and Earth connection, the action and the reaction. I was finally at that stage, whereby I was getting to know myself and what life had in store for me from a deeper truth point of view, understanding why some areas of my life had been so blocked. It was the beginning of the Knowing. The Knowing refers to many stages of knowing, with precognition and such being the later stages. I could safely say I was beginning to know myself, my purpose, and what my life meant, from a place of certainty that resonated throughout my being from up above. It was my new truth, not one that I could mold to suit my alternating states of mind, but one that was irrefutable and anchored in my being, from the eternity of my soul to the atoms vibrating unanimously in my physical vessel. This is what I was conveying to the infant in my arms, from tabula rasa to infinity, all in an instant. This is the first time I am able to write this down, as this book finally enables me to verbalize emotions which until now had been undecipherable in their complexity. I think that by that time, I was beginning to get accustomed to the duality of my life and of my existence on both planes, marked by the contrast between voyages of the soul with the Creator's energy, to the mundane bits of every-day life. There would be obstacles with this new mindset, but the more time passed, the more I was comfortable with the journey. Eventually, the first course ended, and I gave myself a very positive check sign in my mind, and promptly signed on for the next one. This would be a new experience with a more practical and physical energy: Reiki.

Reiki was what I needed at the time to ground all of this etheric energy, even though it took me a long time to get accustomed to using it frequently. It gave me more physical feedback, in regards to my godliness, with the body acting as a vessel for channeling this energy. It is a feminine energy of love, stirring up elements of your physical and spiritual bodies simultaneously. The initiation lasts 21 days, to mimic the

21-day cycle its channeler and "creator" had to go through in Japan in the early 20th century. I believe the most important lesson I learned from this, with time, is the essence and meaning of loving ourselves. This is a tool that brings forth and grounds love for you when you need it most and do not know how to tap into it, an endless source of appreciation for your existence on this planet. I can fully attest to the fact that it works.

It is very soothing, especially when the hand is applied onto the heart chakra, a very relaxing, sedating experience accessible anytime, anywhere, and especially useful in times of distress and anxiety. Love is the message of this book, a gradual entry into the consciousness of this word. Like we can create, we can and must love in order to reach balance in our lives. It is the vessel that carries us through difficult times and enables us to rise again from our perils. It is the light that remains when all is dark. Like hope, it lifts us up even for a brief moment, but enough to instill in us the belief that there exists salvation somewhere beyond our pain. We, unfortunately, attribute great futility to this word, as we reduce it from an infinite concept to a word. None is the wiser as to what it means, other than Valentine's Day and all sorts of romantic characteristics created by modern consumerism. The truth is that in order to love others, we must first take care of number one: US. It is not selfishly motivated, but logically so, as we cannot help others when our own source of living essence is depleted. Otherwise, we would be left empty of whatever energy remained. If you look beyond the word **Love** and recognize it as a necessity for life, you realize that it is essentially fuel for the soul. Taking care of ourselves first is a gradual transition that occurs with a lot of self-reflection. It doesn't have to be lengthy or difficult. It requires us to look within, and ask ourselves truthfully why we do not feel up to par, why we settle on your ideals, embrace mediocrity, and why we judge ourselves so adamantly that, when we are done, all that remains is a shadow of what we once were. This change is meant to empower you, but first you must face your "demons," the parts of yourself that you fear, you must ask why they are present, and what they have to teach you. Everything is a lesson, whether you choose to accept it or not. Coincidence does not exist. The synchronicity we experience from the Universe on a daily basis highlights the complexity of all the elements we come across, that are meant to teach us the lessons we decided to learn in this lifetime. The most important recurring theme here is love. Love is the way to get through this and it is the light that awaits you at the end of your journey. It is the fuel for the way and the hope for when the tank is empty. Accepting who you are as a person, on the outside and in, is the path you have to embrace. Through this acceptance and reconciliation with your reality, you can learn to love yourself in the fullest sense, and ultimately, those around you, and all that encompasses your life. You can and will change your life. You will open up, your body language will change, your smile will widen, and the Universe will repay all this positivity with even more. This is the power of love, available inside of your soul today. All of this is an essential life lesson, and not one I came by easily. It took me perhaps another year and a half to start applying the Reiki to my reality and myself during times of distress, when I had no other tool as immediately effective. It worked its magic and here I am.

The healing is done with the hands as they are applied over the body, meant to stir up all the etheric and physical blockages inside, to rise to the surface and be cleansed. The process is sometimes challenging but always necessary. Many of these arising issues are difficult to deal with, that is why they were buried for so long. They can then manifest in the body as temporary physical ailments, or even in your behavior. This is very temporary a process, but when you want to clean to get to the bottom of something, you must first get rid of the layer of sludge on top. It massages the tissues without touching them and rids them of all the negative thought-patterns that lie therein. Like in astrology, when we see the body manifesting problems in certain areas, what we conclude after assuming that the physical vessel reflects the journey of the soul, is that it indicates what the problem really is on a spiritual level. You can use your body to understand your pain and where it comes from. Ultimately, engaging in behaviors that affect certain areas of your life, like anger in matters of love, would, in turn, manifest in the heart chakra area and cause a real physical problem. Your astrological chart does not tell you that you are susceptible to certain problems. It tells you that your karmic debt and baggage in certain areas of your life may cause you to experience specific physical problems within the related chakra, where it to manifest in the body. Reiki addresses both the physical vessel and its etheric counterpart. I cannot say that it will cure you of anything, unless you are willing to address the source of the problem. It will bring things to the surface and heal the body if you agree to let go, and begin using a newfound, loving perspective as a tool directed towards the affected area/mindset. What is important to highlight about Reiki, the most striking thing it has to offer besides the healing, is the universal symbols. It uses Japanese letters, written in different combinations and projected towards a situation or destination, as a protective and healing instrument. It enables you to project these anywhere, anytime. They essentially act as a conscious shield or vessel for an objective or person, whereby they mark it and it remains under the watchful eye of this energy for a certain amount of time. I remember one young woman I met was telling me that she had been using them for 15 years on her car before driving, and had never had a single mishap. The day that she neglected to do them, she got into an accident. I have been using them for a few years, and can attest to the fact that I feel safe even in the most ludicrous situations, on the road or elsewhere. I can use them in the event that I have an important meeting and I want to arrive balanced and whole. They never fail to deliver in these instances. In some way, they cause an entire domino effect of synchronicity during the day to come, and everything falls into place. This requires me to cancel all my negative thoughts from the day before, and send a wave of white light throughout my future day first. Then, I will couple that with the Reiki symbols, and I am very well covered. Between this and my spirit guides, I always feel like there is a convoy of light with me wherever I go. I realize this is very abstract and esoteric material, but I want to highlight that it is the 5th-dimensional awareness in effect. It is creating at its most tangible. You literally can bring your day into being in a very conscious manner, and avoid all the little pebbles on the way that tend to make a journey uncomfortable. I can attest to the fact that logistics, from commuting, to flights and meetings, now have an uncanny way of mysteriously falling into place for my benefit. It even enables you to leave your home with a minimal amount of money and maneuver throughout the day, getting everything you need down to the last cent in an orderly manner. Some days, I will even get into situations when I picture a number that I would like to pay for something and, if I release that thought as it came without my ego and willpower interfering, it works out exactly as I wished.

This is the ultimate power we have. With a few of these tools, we can begin to taste the ability we have to mold our reality. If it is indeed a matrix of energies and circumstances, it is as malleable as we design it to be. Imagine a complex 3D image on a computer screen. It starts with imaging and mapping and results as a culmination of all the layers that give the designer precisely what he wanted, down to the millimeter. This is your ability as well. It comes gradually, and beyond the external tools available, there are your innate gifts that will awaken with time. Reality is tricky, as it is truly in the eye of the beholder. Everyone lives within a matrix of their own making, and these ultimately twist and intertwine to create the dimensions we live in. We call it reality, but it really looks like myriad dimensions of thought and consciousness superposed on one another to create the one single layer we see with the lenses of our eyes. I believe Reiki should come in at the beginning of a spiritual voyage, as the sheer idea that moving your fingers to mimic an Asian scripture and releasing this to the Universe, could actually return to us in a physical manifestation of safety and perfect synchronicity. It is a beautiful thing. As time passes you get more and more accustomed to it and drop all the skepticism, as you do see the difference between a day with and a day without Reiki. I went through the 21-day initiation, whereby I had to dedicate a good hour and a half every day to covering my whole body with this energy, long after the course was over. I felt elated and more positive. I felt the toxins slowly being pushed out of my cells and my body, a process which was corroborated later by medical tests. I would, much later, go through a new month-long initiation to work on my addictions, which were still anchored in my energy even if I didn't succumb to them anymore.

Addiction in itself is a process of self-loathing, and giving up on ourselves through self-punishment. There is a lot of ego within this pattern, as well as, occasionally, negative entities that have attached themselves to us, but we will cover all that later. I would write on little bits of papers a thank you note to the Reiki and the Creator for healing this part of me, and keep them on me for the entire month, sending them energy when I felt they were "calling." Sure enough, they disappeared, a sign that this process was over. I witnessed mindsets changing with time, where pain once lurked there was now love, and I could alter my thoughts when I went in a negative direction. I had realized just how much, and how simply, this gift could be in our lives. Just like that, the course had ended, and I moved on to another level, a whole new state of consciousness, with new challenges and discoveries.

I then signed up for an intense introduction to channeling. **Channeling** is a dichotomous word. It infers acting as a channel for Spirit as if it speaks through you. This is true in some ways. The second and lesser meaning is that it enables you to listen to the voice within, your truth. If you accept the notion that the Creator is everything all at once and you its energy, then when it speaks through you the voice is ultimately yours, one of its trillion different faces. We only channel or tackle things that are right for us. Perhaps they are not necessarily right for us in ways we directly understand. Nonetheless, we never experience things that we cannot handle, otherwise we would not ultimately be able to learn from them. Incarnation equates lesson. Learn and release is the motto of your life, or so it should be. Unfortunately, unless we are acquainted with this ability to listen inwards, we cannot tap into this knowledge, that gives us cause and effect, and lets us know what it is we are here now to learn and change. Karma does not discriminate. Everyone experiences it, with no exceptions. It is a wheel we have gotten ourselves into as we entered the cycle of Mother Earth, and we are now finally entering a new age when we can be free of these shackles and start anew. All of this requires the ability to listen. Our Higher Self, our Soul, our Angelic guardians, the Creator, and even some benevolent extraterrestrials are always watching and guiding us. In this, they also make no exceptions. This is the nature of equality. They all consider us to be equal in our right to exist and experience free will. It is not to say that some people with specific tasks that benefit humanity are not given extra care to make sure they awaken at the right time, but the truth is that most do not fulfill their obligations in their given lifetime. The key is again to listen.

We often cannot hear our guidance directly, but only through thoughts and decisions we believe to be our own. If we embrace these and they resonate with our truth, then we are able to make positive life choices, and take the enlightened path. There is always the right to choose, but your guides watch over you and try to point you in the right direction every moment of your lives. Therefore, channeling can really help save you so much trouble, as you learn straight away what is right for you. One thing is imperative to highlight here: the ability to channel is innate in every single living being, and so is telepathy. We call it déjà vu or coincidence when we think of someone and the phone rings the same instant. There is no coincidence. We use the word intuition among many others. It is none of these. It is as inherent as breathing, with no exceptions. We often choose to go and see psychics and mediums, and we empower them with messages that pertain to us. Many times, their minds or egos can meddle with the message, and yet, we still revere them. There is only one person that we must put on a pedestal: ourselves. Channeling brings the ball back into our court, so to speak. It empowers us with a message from our own truth, and connects us with our ultimate purpose. A good and impartial teacher is essential during this journey, but this is again a conscious choice we make. If we really agree, on a soul level, to learn this in the purest and cleanest way without misuse, but because we are searching for a truth that pertains to us above all others, we find that we must acquiesce to finding the most perfect energetic match. I have met many people that feared this notion, and that believed it was ungodly, wrong and fraudulent. Some believed it would disrupt the balance of the heavens, others were comfortable with the notion of God as an omnipotent, judgmental being, who works in mysterious ways, living beyond the clouds and speaking through prophets.

I believe it is not only the right thing, but a necessity, for one to understand what God is from within. It is you, you are God. That is a bold and presumptuous statement for most. For this reason, I wish to make a differentiation. I have noted, to my amusement, that when I would mention the word God, or Elohim in Hebrew, the faces of fear and awe people would make. God of the 21ˢᵗ century is an intangible concept, so far beyond our grasp that we are humbled by it, and fearful of its wrath. We do not honestly believe that we would be able to hear or speak to him. Our holy texts portray him as a judgmental archetype of all-that-is, that casts plagues, and tests men constantly. If we do not understand what is happening, we will simply conclude that he works in mysterious ways. Now, I do not want to make this about religion since it is not, and I respect the right of every living being on this planet to their own opinion. The very worrying notion that I want to highlight here is the fact that, through all of these ideals, we have now removed from ourselves any responsibility for what happens to this planet and the people on it. We can all agree that man follows a certain course of action that can be "good" or "bad," and that would be reflected by the consequences of his actions, and the society we live in. On the religious front, this would ultimately be a reflection of good and evil.

If someone were to be in a compromising situation, it would be as a consequence of acting in a certain way, a judgment on who he or she is by the very stern notion of right and wrong. This is highly detrimental to our existence. There is one thing to learn from this: in the circle of life, whereby the difficulties we face are defined by the karma we chose for ourselves, we are solely responsible for all the situations we encounter, for "good" or for "bad." We can create through fear, anger, or through balancing and clearing our karmic debt. We thus hold the keys. We are the alpha and the omega, the action and the consequence, the beginning and the end. This is the notion that we do not want to accept as a species: when all goes wrong, we shall have to point the finger at the person in the mirror. This would indeed be difficult, but if we pray or ask for forgiveness and immerse ourselves in doctrine, we get as far away from the objective as possible. Were we to accept that we have attracted or created this situation, we would then ask the next logical question: "What am I supposed to learn from this?" By asking why you have chosen this for yourself on some level or another, you can leave the pity and fear behind, learn, and try to resolve it. Solely this way can we address our problems and stop blaming them on external influences. The bottom line is that what we call God does not meddle in our lives on any level. It only created the cosmic laws I will cover later, the most important being **"Freedom of Choice."** Everything is your choice, a creation of your own making, and the sooner you accept this fact, the sooner you can begin to address your issues. This means as much for someone with a very stern image of God, as for someone with a totally atheistic point of view, who believes everything is an evolutionary consequence and that life is a collection of random occurrences that have no meaning or pattern. I, by no means, want to infringe on your right to choose. It is the only thing that keeps us relatively free at the moment. What I offer is a change of attitude. I propose to change the word God into the Creator. It is a change of notion, a Creator that is nothing more or nothing less than an infinite, sentient consciousness. I don't believe we can really grasp it in any other way. It has no face, no gender and no archetype. It is the pure energy of love. If you wish to see it, look in the mirror, as you are its reflection. I strongly believe that to understand this energy we would have to unite every single subatomic and atomic particle in the **Multiverse** (all dimensions of the Universe combined) and everything in between, including black holes and vortexes. Even then, it would not encompass it all, as there are things that we simply cannot fathom at this time. The Creator speaks to each of us through our own voice. We are the many tentacles of its being, its different faces, and in that, we are all equal in our right to exist. It loves us all equally and considers us its children. It is unconditional love, existing above anger, resentment and ego. It simply empowers us with light and free will, in order to assume our role as Creators. Afterwards, we are on our own path to evolve, like a merger of Creationism and Evolution. This is the beauty of diversity in the unexpected array of configurations we see in nature, all the way down to our society. We are all basically the same, yet we manage to be so utterly different: our clothing, the music we listen to, the colors we surround ourselves with, the dogmas we adopt, the melanin concentration of our skin, the morphology of our physique, and the belief systems we hold. They are all illusions. Universes apart when, under the surface, we are all reflections of each other. We live in pluralistic societies where we coexist without, on the most part, killing each other, and we are slowly realizing that we are one sentient being when we must rely on each other. Find the most improbable match for you, sit with them, and after a few minutes you will realize that underneath all the masks, the socio-economic status, the languages and innuendos, you are simply brothers and sisters. That is the Creator speaking through you, reminding you through this flicker of emotion who you are meant to be. If all energy came from one source and broke down into infinite particles, at the source it is still inherently the same. This is the nature of All-That-Is, a cornucopia of all living beings, physical and spiritual. Therefore, why diminish the individual and attribute his power of Self to another man or woman, when they are all basically distributed energies of the exact same source? Therein lies the essence of the Creator, it gives to you all that it is and does not pretend to be more or less than you, since it is you. Here we find the inherent difference with our modern God archetype which hasn't changed much since the days of yore, when he was judgmental and all-powerful, when his wrath was what men ultimately feared, and when he tested your faith in whatever way he saw fit. I believe that to enter a new age of awareness, we not only have to revise and refresh our spiritual foundations, but perhaps to look at the Source in a more modern, open-minded manner. This is the only way we can grasp what it means to tell us when it speaks directly through us, even though we are mostly unaware of the provenance of this knowledge. Despite all being linked to this source of infinite love, we mostly communicate with it in a semi-conscious manner when we are asleep or inattentive. Many things we perceive as dreams are actually complex messages pertaining to our lives, that we are meant to decipher and understand. When we debate on an issue that matters to us, the resolve we acquire through reflection comes in thought-form from our guidance or the Creator, like a telepathic universal message. The basis of channeling is doing that consciously and tapping into the waves of knowledge that are directed our way, and decrypting them through our own words and conscious mind.

To perceive what the Universe is in essence, we must picture **vibration**. Everything vibrates at its own frequency. When I was a teenager, I had a math tutor who was also an accomplished cello player. He always demonstrated to me, in different ways, that everything has its own tone and vibration that it resonates with. Make a certain pitch on an instrument or even with your voice, and see a certain piece of furniture vibrate while others do not, according to density. This corresponds exactly to what we are addressing here. We all are making a transition from 3rd to 5th density. The higher we move up in dimensions, the more we evolve in awareness and the less dense we become, both in attitude and physical constitution. We will never notice it, since there is no measuring instrument at the moment that can quantify this, and we are so accustomed to our physical constitution that many of the changes are trivial to our sensory system. Besides this, we all have our personal vibratory frequency that coincides with our spiritual awareness. Being that everything is made up of energy that vibrates at different frequencies, and that all physical beings are manifestations of spiritual consciousness, our own vibratory frequencies are non-local. They exist everywhere and nowhere simultaneously. The communication between these is made possible through the translation of a specific vibratory energy into a message. This happens as you communicate with the consciousness of your choice and they respond with said frequency. It is then laid out into a message, deciphered by your consciousness and put into your own words. If you ever desired to somehow picture the spiritual world as it really is, you would see different waves of consciousness floating in an endless sea of energy, perhaps in different hues or colors to distinguish them, and communicating via frequencies and vibrations that would probably make quite a beautiful sound. The images we have of spiritual beings, such as the Archangel Michael as a human figure with a shield and golden wings as he is often portrayed, are only anthropomorphized visions according to archetypes, so that we may accept and process them. The truth is that they are nameless, genderless, without any appellation, separated only by their different vibrations and densities. There is indeed a very clear hierarchy between all of these, whether they are etheric extraterrestrials, human souls, or souls belonging to the Angelic hierarchy. They are classified according to what beings were created first, their purpose, and their ability to withstand the light of the Creator, its immense vibratory frequency. The closer they are to it, the more they are branded Angelic, and enter the different

strata of these beings, like the Seraphim, Cherubim, etc...
as per Jewish, Christian and Muslim eschatological dogma. I
understood this with time through channeling, that we must
step out of our comfort zone if we really want to see the true
face of things. They are more abstract than I could have ever
imagined, but I do relish the challenge of accepting new and
disruptive ideas. I must say that the sheer fact that we can
obtain knowledge from the Creator, the one we have yearned
for so long, the one we turn to when our days darken and we
begin to lose hope, and ultimately receive the most subjec-
tively beneficial information for our lives, is the greatest gift
one could ever get. This is not only because we can get the
highest and most enlightened guidance for all that we seek,
but since we feel that connection in our entire being, know
that we are now safe, and that we may always ask for help.
This empowers us as human beings more than anything else.
It brings our essence back and blends it with our physical
vessels, so that we may be complete once again by walking
this Earth knowing who we are, our history, our purpose, and
above all, the nature of universal love that it feels for us. This
is infinity entering our sphere of existence and embracing us
in our entirety, it is us becoming **quantum**, by existing on all
planes, and empowered by their energies.

I cannot say that I was ever fearful of channeling as a concept. I always secretly yearned for the knowledge that is so
evasive in our modern world. Some people I spoke to along
this time expressed fear, but could not rationalize it. Sure, it
was something unattainable and abstract, something we cannot see or grasp, so perhaps we surrender to fear. It is one

thing for someone to channel for us, sort of distancing us from the objective as we face a person. It is another when that voice and that energy speaks to us and we feel it within, as if we faced ourselves from the abyss of our souls.

The day I stepped into this course I knew I was doing the right thing. I had longed for this since the nights of my childhood, when, sad and sleepless, I would look out my window and speak to my idea of God, telling him I wanted to go home, and I would do so if he only provided me with one truth, one revelation about the world. I would be ready to leave this plane and go wherever if only I knew. I didn't know if he existed or if there was something out there, but I believed that beyond the endless sky were secrets we couldn't imagine, and I wanted to tap into that knowledge. Little did I know that one day, without giving anything up, I would live in between worlds as I entered my mid-twenties.

The course itself was comforting. There were familiar faces and new ones, but the atmosphere was supportive and loving. We were given an introduction to channeling. I knew much about it by now from my teacher, who had been giving me messages in past lifetime regressive therapy sessions. The first empowering thing I remember was a guided meditation where we were asked to go into our own vision of nature by walking along a path, and describe what we saw. The surroundings and animals along the way all signified something about us, which we would decipher afterwards. Everything had a meaning, and it was to show us that we basically always channeled, even without knowing it. As I fell deeper into a trance, I found myself in an endless forest of Sequoia trees, gargantuan in size. There was a white snake along the path. I was then met by a deer who guided me to the edge of the forest. Behind the dense line of trees lay a blanket of white, a blinding white endless line. A great, tall man, dressed in white, with a long white beard greeted me and took me on a journey into the endless white background. We scaled a hill on a train and then entered a tunnel, accompanied by a great brown bear. At the top of the hill was a white door. They bid me farewell and opened the door. I crossed the threshold and gained consciousness again. It was vivid and encouraging but I didn't really know what it meant. Later, as I met with A and told her the vision, I could spot the surprise in her eyes as it seemed this was unprecedented. The forest represented the number of lifetimes and knowledge acquired, which was as immense as the trees. The deer represented spiritual guidance, and the snake healing powers and knowledge. The part that came afterwards was of surprise. It was obvious the tall man was a figure of the Creator. I do not remember what the bear signified. The appearance of this human figure within the lights, the ascending journey and the door, were synonymous with an ancient soul that had come from very high and was going to return there. My teacher's eyes lit up in a way that was significant, and I understood that this was going to be an interesting ride. I was beginning to understand certain things she had told me during our sessions. I was an Indigo Child, a very old soul. This was one of my few physical incarnations as I had been mostly incarnated in spirit. I had encountered lifetimes in Ancient Egypt and the Mayan culture, as well as

Atlantis and Lemuria. I was well acquainted with dimensions and the Angelic kingdom, and had a very high purpose on this planet at this time, though it was not clear what. At the conclusion of our Reiki course, she had relayed a message to me that I was very close to our Mother Earth, Gaia, and that this was a main part of my karma and purpose here, to heal her by acting as a conduit for the new energies. Since I came from an elevated dimension in the spiritual world, though it was not clear from where, I could withstand extremely powerful energies and channel them directly from the Source. I absorbed all these things, but since I was a novice in this domain, I still had my healthy skepticism. Only a year prior, I was a nihilistic substance abuser that doubted everything. I sniggered on the inside as I wondered what I would have thought if I had been exposed to all of this 5 years earlier. I probably would have chased this idea away like a solicitor. Yet, we change, just like the world does. The Universe is in a constant state of flux, along with everything in it. We usually do not notice it in until, in retrospect, we ponder about how our lives changed drastically at certain points in time. The bottom line is that I was here because of a sign from above, and I felt the chips falling into place, so I thought I might as well continue on this journey.

We followed by going through some secretive initiations, basically branding us as vessels for channeling, opening up the official connections that had been closed for so long. I remember fondly during one of our meditations, being snapped out of whatever we were doing, and going into a universal vortex that led me to the **Central Sun of the Universe**, even though I did not know what that meant. I ended up there, looking up from within the matrix of space, at a cloud of soft white energy with a huge light emanating from it. It told me that it was waiting for me to return home. I still remember the hairs on my entire body standing up. I later found out that the Central Sun is another name for the concentration of the Source energy, sort of a non-local place where the energy emanates from. At least, that is the most feasible explanation for such an enormous and nebulous idea. When we later went through a formal initiation that connected us to the Creator's light, I understood what it meant. We were put into a meditative state and told we would experience a reconnection with the Creator. I remember seeing a sort of link between Heaven and Earth coming throughout my crown chakra and reaching up towards the light, being reconnected, like a severed ligament sewn back together. I was told this "thread" was the "Tree of Life," Etz Hahaim in Hebrew, even though I had no idea what that meant. When it was reunited, I started moving upwards throughout this vortex, through layers of infinity. Eventually, I reached a place that I still use in my meditations. I call it my placid lake. I was standing in a grayish landscape of mountains and a lake, with a clear sky above. Everything seemed real but made of crystal somehow. I was told this was the Creator. I was prompted to keep moving upwards until I braced a white membrane of sorts. As soon as I crossed it, I found myself in an endless sea of blinding light, where top was indistinguishable from bottom. This was the crown chakra of the Creator. It was totally ludicrous but my entire being vibrated with this experience, so that it was difficult to argue with the inner feeling that this was right, more right than anything else I had ever experienced. Eventually, I saw my form as a baby-like hue of white, as I peered into a giant white eye. I sat down in the lotus position and eventually I blended with the white background until I was gone. Said eye is a symbol for spiritual guidance, especially if it is blue, and it would become synonymous with visions of the Creator and my guides. It is used often in mysticism, especially on talismans against the evil eye around the Mediterranean and the Middle East. By now, I was very pleased with the channeling course. I was finally waking up to my abilities. It was fruitful and we increasingly experienced the ability to channel, for now with shapes and glyphs, approaching the day when we would do it through words.

That day eventually came and I was eager and enthused to finally get clear messages from my guidance and be able to communicate with them directly, without a middleman. We first experienced a trial with our guides to identify themselves, and to learn how to distinguish their voices. It was hearing or "seeing" by telepathy, exactly like the sound of a thought. I still remember myself trying to. Everything was blocked, I became flustered and frustrated. Eventually, I exploded and had to go outside for a break. I had reached the pinnacle of my studies and hit a blank. I was so utterly angry with everything and needed to vent. That day everyone received their first verbal message, while I got mine in shapes and signs. The course soon finished and I was still not able to breach that blockage, but my teacher assured me everything would be fine. I was frankly embarrassed and angry, out of pure frustration. Time went by, perhaps a few weeks, and I meditated at night trying to get a clear message, but it was all enigmatic triangles and eyes.

I was invited by a friend who was a healer and yoga teacher to go up to Haifa, a northern coastal city, for a group session. I had met this man I will call Y through his brother, and told he was a healer. I had discovered that he employed a very physical machine that used frequencies for diagnostics and healing. It was similar to a Royal Rife Frequency machine, but more advanced. Frequency Medicine uses the principle of vibration. Just like every piece of furniture in your house can vibrate at a different frequency, the same can be said about organs in the body, down to the smallest detail. This apparatus would scan your body with frequencies through electrodes attached to your feet. These would, incredibly, be able to map out your entire body in about half an hour. The machine had recorded the frequencies of different parts of the body and could scan where there was energy lacking, just like the negative of a picture in contrast to the regular image. It then sent the correct frequencies to the affected parts to balance and replenish the energy as needed. The organs would be filled with their own frequency until they achieved homeostasis. I must say that as a diagnostic tool, it was able to identify everything, including toxins and pesticides from within the cell itself, and would then list homeopathic remedies that could help with the imbalance. I still remember it identifying calcium carbonate in my body, meaning the Tums that I had taken the night before, all through a frequency! A cup of coffee meant an overactive adrenal system, or meditating throughout the session meant a stimulated pituitary gland i.e. the crown chakra. I also remember laughing while seeing that a medication I was taking, usually foreign to the body since it is a chemical substance, being marked as the only safe thing in the list of toxins after I had administered Reiki symbols to it. The most alien element with the best energy: what a laughable idea! That specific day turned out to be a breakthrough for me. The machine temporarily raises the frequency of the body, so I was perhaps attaining a 5th dimension vibratory level for an hour. I was beating myself up over something while under treatment with this machine, before the kundalini yoga class. Suddenly, out of the chaos of my thoughts, I heard a very concise and clear voice. He identified himself as the **Metatron**, telling me everyone evolved at their own pace, and that he had been waiting for me for a long time. He announced that he would be my guide from now on. I was so elated with this renewed ability. I cherished that moment and now felt assured that everything was going to be fine. The yoga session was mind-opening, and I was able to reach new levels of meditation. That day I understood that I had been channeling throughout the entirety of the courses I had followed, as well as most of my conscious life. I had just made a grave mistake. I had expected fireworks and revelations in channeling. I believed I would physically hear voices and see things immediately. It was not so. Only seldom did things manifest themselves in that manner, when people would have otherwise not been able to understand them. The voice was my own, like that of a thought, just much crisper and directed at me. I could distinguish it and understand where it came from, but it was a far cry from what I had expected from channeling. I was momentarily saddened as I had been channeling all along, disregarding the subtle nature of a message as a thought, and making my life more difficult. That was over now, and it was time to tune in. Channeling is always there, during our entire lives. The question is whether we listen or not. It is like tuning a radio. The message exists on several frequencies in a muffled form, but only on one as a clear and direct version. That is precisely what we do when begin to channel. We listen to our inner voice relaying messages to us, by tuning into these. Even the words are our own. The original form is energy, then translated through our current form and colloquialism, personality, in English, French, etc... We then get the message as though it was a thought and we understand it as ours. It is simply that, no matter where it comes from.

Now, the Metatron exists apparently only in Christianity, in the books of Enoch. Meta means after, and tron means matrix, in ancient Greek. He exists beyond the Matrix that separates us from the Creator, and is thought to be an ascended Master that now holds the energy of Seraph, and is the highest ranking and closest being to the Creator. Ancient texts refer to him as Enoch. Along with Elijah, he had reached such a high level of spiritual awareness that, upon his passing, he was able to become an Ascended Master (a human soul that had reached the pinnacle of spirituality for itself) and take his place beside the Creator. It is said that Enoch and Elijah, now known as Metatron and Sandalphon, are the only two human beings to have achieved this. Metatron is able to channel to

Creator's light as much as possible for any being aside from the Creator himself. This was the beginning of a new stage of awareness for me, as I was now firmly anchored in my new faith and knew that, despite the outlandish experience I now called life, it was as real as anything else I knew, and it was an integral part of my existence.

As I began my new life as a human being existing on both planes with full awareness, I reflected on what channeling really meant, especially with the Creator. I realized how ludicrous it sounded if you said you could speak to God, if people realized there were many groups on the globe that entertained the notion of doing so daily. This is why I really wanted to coin him the Creator. The word God was long lost, as it was programmed into people's minds as an ultimate, unattainable deity, and nothing could change that. You would have to be liberated from that thought process to even accept the true nature of the Creator. Living in Israel at the time, religion was everywhere. I imagined a Hassidic Jew, so plunged into his doctrine, being presented with the notion that the being that he has worshipped his entire life, whose name he dared not pronounce, would address someone directly without all the prayer and ritualism. He would find it upsetting and asinine. The God concept was too far embedded in his psyche for him to perceive it as anything else than what he had been taught. Sadly, this does not only apply to people of faith, but agnostics as well, or occasional churchgoers. I put off this book and dedicating myself to what I had learned because I imagined the collective consciousness, in Israel and beyond, having difficulty entertaining this notion. What about the fact that this wasn't about me or those I studied with, but a universal idea, accessible by ANYONE? Still hard to swallow. With time, I called him the Creator and the attitude changed, people were less afraid. Yet, the minute the word God entered a discussion you could feel the attitude subversively changing. I still find it amusing that people have no problem believing that angels, demons, extraterrestrials, and all sorts of other crypto-zoological species could be part of their lives, affecting them directly, but not God. If I mentioned the Archangels and their messages, people accepted and reflected, but as soon as the mighty G word appeared, the air was electrified with resistance. Luckily, with time and my making peace with who I am, I was able to accept that what was right for others would enter their lives when it was time, and that people could surprise you at the most unexpected times. I have changed my notion of God, and time will tell what it will seed, but I meet more and more people that seem to have shed their preconceptions, and are ready to entertain something new. At the Source there is only one energy, and we are all creators.

The minute I could channel, I could explore the spiritual world as much as I wanted, whereby the sky was literally not the limit anymore. A new world was available to me, possibilities were totally limitless, and I was very happy about this renewed ability. This was open me up to a new way of living, communicating with beings from other dimensions, universes and planetary systems, both physical and etheric. I was still reading and absorbing information, and I knew that there was much for me to learn. I had always had a profound desire to unravel the world of what we called ETs, intelligence from other planets. I now knew they existed, from my own readings, as well as my teacher's. This was an enigma as big as the number of planets in our known universe. There were literally infinite possibilities and configurations of worlds where humanoid beings lived, some totally different from us. This is what I could conclude from what I knew. Little did I understand that if I wanted to picture them I should only have to go, for the most part, to the mirror. The technique we had learned in channeling enabled me to filter out all that was not right for me to communicate with, and to do it only through my guidance and the Creator. This was very import-ant as there are many interplanetary and interdimensional be-ings out there that are not benevolent. When I would explore this world at the beginning, not knowing where to begin, I would do it exclusively through the Creator, asking for what was right to come my way.

I had contact with beings seemingly from Antares at that time. I was still getting used to channeling, so I sometimes had, especially when it came to new names and star systems, difficulty identifying them. The one that struck me the most was Yahweh, or Jehovah as he called himself. He seemed very benevolent. It would be many months before we were reunit-ed and I understood who he was and what he had to teach me. The basis of it was that, despite the fact that I thought he was from Antares, he was an etheric angelic being from the 10th Dimension from a group called the Founders, the first physical beings ever created before time existed. They were once exactly like us and had evolved to the point that they were no longer in physical form. They guided other civilizations, physical and etheric, and called themselves the Elohim. They were often confused for God by our spiritual leaders, as Elohim in Hebrew is God. The truth is that it is the plural form of El, inferring that there is more than one. I would be contacted by them later, when I was more mature and had learned to identify my ego and communicate without it, but not before they left me with a present. By now, I had only experienced this world in a spiritual sense, through my mind's eye/third eye and my intuition, but I had not yet seen something clearly that I could put my finger on. There were sometimes shadows or shapes around me, but I could still rationalize in my mind that they were nothing. One evening, I was running from the National Park of Tel-Aviv next to the safari, on my way home, iPod resounding through my ears and my heart rate elevated from the jogging. I was thinking very deeply about Yahweh and imagining a meeting with him and the eventual revelation to the human collective consciousness about the spirit world. At that time, I did not really know who he was or what his story was, but he projected a very warm and positive energy, so I went with it. I knew I had only to ask for the protection of the Metatron or the Creator, even though they were always present. Out of the corner of my left eye came a ball of fire. I turned my head slightly and saw a meteor-like "ball" of red with a yellowish flame, appearing out of the sky across from the freeway and landing in a schoolyard. The adrenaline started pumping in my system, tears in my eyes and hairs erect all over my body. I froze. The earphones fell out of my ears. I began to look around, aghast. I started to walk across the freeway without looking at the oncoming traffic. I was conscious that it had happened, but it is something to feel and something else to see. I walked over to the school in a trance, jumping over the gate, looking for the "meteor." I found nothing at all. It had apparently appeared as it had disappeared. I had a grin on my face as I realized this was a new stage in my spiritual evolution. As I made my way home and began to channel, Yahweh greeted me and told me that I had experienced an electromagnetic vibration which had produced this wave of color. I honestly have no idea as to the science of it all, but all the skepticism and rationalizing in me were dumbfounded. I was of sound mind and sane, and yet I had seen the impossible. I could not argue any longer as to the reality of the other "reality. " Yahweh left me to my learning process, as I enriched myself and got ready for our next encounters.

Along the same time, I had learned about the Lemurians. Many of my discoveries were done through random errands which would, by chance, lead me to a bookstore with a metaphysical section where I would encounter a manuscript calling out to me, only to communicate with the energies or beings it was about later that day. I must say that my curiosity is boundless and I have always had a thirst for knowledge, even today, constantly researching, reading, and wanting more.

Through the book "Revelations of the New Lemuria, Telos Vol 1" by Aurelia Louise Jones, I discovered the world of Lemuria. I had already experienced Atlantis and Lemuria for myself through visions of past lives, but this offered the notion that, as Atlantis and Lemuria eventually vanished, survivors from Atlantis left for Egypt, Tibet, and South America, while the Lemurians went underground. The timetable is vague, but Lemuria came first. It is my understanding that the first beings to populate this planet came to be after the seeds of our DNA were planted by benevolent extraterrestrials eons ago. The planet had always been visited by entities from other planets and dimensions. There are also some native to Earth, or Terra as it is called. They are not necessarily benevolent but we are safe from them so I will not dwell on this issue. The story of Terra and man is one that binds Creationism and Evolution. We were seeded and left to evolve. So, they are both existent. Many of our civilizations come from different places according to the DNA they possess. We were originally our ape ancestors, but with genetic alterations we were able to suddenly evolve, approximately 100,000 years ago, and become the people we are today. Eventually, the Cro-Magnon starts to mysteriously disappear, followed by the Neanderthal, and Homo Sapiens Sapiens come into being. Before all this, there was a period called Hyperborea, probably coinciding with the era of the dinosaurs. These were the first incarnations, and humanoid beings came in all shapes. Since consciousness is immortal, there was an attempt at finding a vessel for the soul that would suit these conditions. Everything was much larger in size at that time. Millions of years later, modern humans were seeded, infused with DNA of light that would cause us to evolve, not only physically, but to reach a higher state of awareness. It is very Descartian in nature, that a thinking creature realizes it is partaking in this experience we call life by the sheer fact that it finds itself thinking and reflecting on its own existence. This awareness, despite initially being limited, is what separates us from our simian cousins and most other species on this planet. It is essentially the Creator Seed, whereby light and consciousness elevate us to our current status as creators and explorers.

Lemuria was the first organized civilization on this planet and spanned tens of thousands of years. It was highly spiritually advanced, very agricultural, and connected to Gaia. The Atlanteans, who emerged later and lasted until before the Great Pyramid of Giza was built, were lower in density, less spiritual, and much more technologically oriented. Their innovations and advancements rival, by far, the best technology we have today. They started out as a break-off from Lemuria and thus had the same values, but declined with time and succumbed to greed and fear. At a certain time, both societies existed in parallel and went to war, creating very negative karma that we are clearing today. They were eventually both destroyed by nature and man, and sank beneath the sea. Atlantis spanned across the Atlantic Ocean, from Gibraltar, through the Azores, all the way to South America. The remnants of this civilization gave way to the Mayas and the Aztecs in South America and the Egyptians Dynasties, as well as pre-Babylonian civilizations from Asia Minor to Tibet. They are the reason we see ziggurats and pyramidal structures from Giza to Machu Picchu, the Balkans, the Yucatan Peninsula, Ur in Mesopotamia, and South Eastern Asia. I studied history in college and remember leaving with more questions than I had answers. I was told that we were to report history, not ask questions, but I was dumbfounded at the sheer amount of archaeological evidence that uprooted the many theories the historical institutions of today have about the beginning of man. Endless sites in Giza, Malta, Tixuanaco, Easter Island, and Yonaguni, are all still unanswered enigmas. I remember the age of the Great Pyramid of Giza finally being changed when they realized it was much older than previously concluded, perhaps as far back as 12500 BC. What did this say about the capabilities of man then? No answer. The three pyramids were constructed to mimic Orion's belt. These huge blocks were aligned so well that you couldn't enter a piece of paper between them, and the construction of diagonal pathways going to the main chamber throughout the structure wouldn't be feasible even today without steel structures. All these, and more, had puzzled me until recently when I opened my eyes. These enigmas screamed Atlantis and Lemuria, but no one heard the cry. I wondered why there were such beautiful texts written about them in the 19th century, from Theosophists and scholars, and suddenly, as we reached the middle of the 20th century, all these theories disappeared into oblivion and mockery. A look into Ignatius L. Donelly's "Atlantis: The Antediluvian World," from 1882, is a start. "The Story of Atlantis and the Lost Lemuria," by Charles Webster Leadbeater and William Scott Elliot from 1896, is another. Nonetheless, modern historical understandings developed the way they wished, and have selectively chosen what they want to portray, not what really is. This is unfortunate. Atlantis has had a profound effect on the way we are today, but I do not believe it is necessary to elaborate on this in depth since there are seas of information out there for you to dive into. The Lemurians are more significant to me, as they still exist and are actively highly spiritual. They once lived on an area that existed in the Pacific Ocean, spanning across Polynesia, Hawaii, and Easter Island, all the way to New Zealand. These islands are the remnants of this once great land, the highest points of the topography that didn't disappear beneath the ocean tides. All the biblical allusions to the Great Flood pertain to these times, when all was lost except the select few survivors who restarted society in new locations. It is true that the waters engulfed parts of the Mediterranean, especially the island of Santorini in Greece, during the fall of Atlantis. Therefore, it is commonly mistaken for Atlantis itself and its fall. There were indeed always colonies of these two civilizations, and perhaps some existed in Europe.

After the fall of Lemuria, the remaining survivors, who were of the 5th density awareness as opposed to 4th and then 3rd from Atlantis, fled underground into a network of tunnels. The modern story of the Lemurians under Mt. Shasta comes from this. They now exist in a parallel 5th dimension reality, underneath our Earth, in an underground city called Telos which has extensions to the 4 corners of the globe through tunnels. Their leader is called Rana Mu. Their high priest is Adama. Some other characters may arise in channeling, such as Agartha. The night after I discovered this book, I had my first channeling with them. I was very cordially greeted and shown their world, a multi-level, subterranean agricultural society that has an artificial sun and looks like it would on the surface. They often visit the world above incognito, as do so many species of ETs. They look exactly like us even though they are larger in dimensions and encompass, like in Atlantis, all the races and ethnic groups we have today. Their only living descendants on the surface are people of Polynesian lineage such as the Maori, and the Aborigines of Australia. They were very kind and we spoke frequently over the next few days. I was eager to meet them one day. They told me that it would take time for me to reach 5th density awareness to be able to visit them and be on the same frequency, so as not to disturb their energy. In due time, when I had worked on balancing my ego and I was ready and grounded within 5th density awareness, I was very welcome to do so.

The truth is that I had no idea how much I would have to work on myself, addressing my problems, balancing my masculine and feminine sides, my ego, my willpower, and all the elements that were to arise, in order to get to the stage they were referring to. Today, I begin to comprehend this as I am no longer pressed, having understood the continuity of time and unfolding events. I am positive that everything comes when it is right, not when we instantly will it. It has taken me a long time to be able to accept that everything we experience is arranged in order. On one side, we create our own reality, on the other, things are pre-aligned. The reason for this being, and many of my different guides have stressed this, the nature of time. Its fabric unites past, present, and future into one. As I have mentioned before, this enables us to view any given time in our incarnation cycle, the current one and any prior, and even clear past events so as to alter their impact on our current reality. The thing about the 5th dimension is that it exists beyond time. Time is no longer the same. We can begin sensing it from now as it has sped up, so to speak. The idea here is to understand that everything happens for a reason in this continuum. We must alter the importance we put on adhering to strict timeframes, as they are malleable beyond our comprehension. Time itself, encompassing past, present, and future, infers that what will happen has already happened, and what has already happened is happening, so that the three "timezones" are all occurring simultaneously **NOW.** Regarding the NOW, it can be the past, present, or future now. Therefore, it is an illusion. This coincides with creating our reality, in the sense that what we are creating has already been created, and therefore the direction we are on in the present, actively building layer by layer, already exists. This is the reason for precognition and déjà vu. Thus, we create as Creators in the present NOW, while everything has ultimately been laid out and already exists in the future NOW. Therefore, are we really doing anything in the NOW? If we can view the future NOW and see what we are responsible for creating, is it really by choice since we already know the upcoming sequence of events? This is the dichotomous nature of time. It frankly puzzles me even today, and there has been a lot of emphasis on explaining this to me, mostly by ETs and Angelic guides. I have learned to simply accept it. To conclude, I am secure in the NOW, that what is happening is meant to happen, and that what will happen will unfold the way it is supposed to in the continuum that is my lifetime. It is puzzling only at times when my ego feels threatened that it is a pawn in this sequence, and really has no say. My Higher Self, basically a future version of me (we all have them), will then let me know that everything is in place and that as far as it concerns me, there is only the **NOW**. This is the great lesson. I vaguely remember a proverb by an Asian elder, perhaps a Tibetan monk. It basically said that the past is gone, so there is no point in worrying about it, and that the future hasn't happened yet, therefore it is out of our control. In essence, there is only the NOW. If we connect this idea with the conscious creation of our reality, we realize that we can only create by the moment, bit by bit, and eventually all these bits become a lengthy road we look back on in the far future. Only then, can we understand the importance of every building block. This is what we are meant to learn here, although it took me long to decipher it. If we unconsciously create reality out of fear and insecurities and suffer the consequences, the root of this is that ultimately, we never stop worrying about the future. By the time we get to it, we have never lived in the moment, but we have ensured the creation of very negative circumstances in the future NOW. This happened through the accumulation of fearful NOWs. I can personally attest that my greatest successes have come after going to sleep at night and releasing all my baggage pertaining to the future, whether a day or a decade, to my guidance and letting them handle it. I came to understand that to ensure I take care of my building blocks, I must cater to them one by one, in order to make for a smoother path. The future is too far away for me to tackle it, and I frankly do not know what circumstances will come my way. This is the entire notion of the NOW. It is addressed in many esoteric doctrines and is of the utmost importance when we want to really change our habits, and be able to enjoy ourselves and the gifts we possess. I believe that if we cater to the moment and only that, we preserve our health and sanity. Before we know it, we are in another moment and we still maintain that positivity. Addressing the NOW is the key to happiness and we must ask ourselves if we are truly happy and fulfilled in this NOW, or if we are waiting for better days. What can we do to improve today, so that we do not sit and let it slip away while we await to-morrow? If we succeed, by the time dawn sets in, we are no longer waiting but relishing the sensation. I was always the most calculating and future-oriented person. I lived in a cloud of self-criticism and doubt, always picking at myself for not being good enough, and I let many moments slip away in the process. Later on, I was picking at myself for letting these slip away, and the cycle continued. Today, I understand that if I look at my life in retrospect, everything has led me to this moment, like a chain of dominoes. Yet, I could never have planned anything since only the most unpredictable of things happened along the way. Therefore, I know I will be just fine, as it resounds in my heart chakra, and I forgo all desire to know, control, and mold events far, far away. I accept there are only these words that exist in this moment, and that is all. I count this as my most valuable lesson to date, and I thank the Creator for having taught it to me at such a young age.

Another introduction which I hold very dear to me to this day is to my beloved "space brothers" from Arcturus. This ex-perience came when I had finished my studies at the spiritual center and was out on my own, exploring under the guidance of my etheric family. It was a winter day. I remember my cell phone had stopped working. I was quite angry at this, since today it is such a necessity. My guides knew this was important to me, and that I literally could not "live" without it. Yet, everything happens for a reason. I made my way down to the center of Tel-Aviv to get to the service and repair center. It was late afternoon, so I was sure to have the joy of sitting there by the hours with half of the city and their damaged wireless paraphernalia. Safe to say, I was not pleased. As I got there, I was given a number. I had such a long waiting line in front of me that I left, and went for a lengthy stroll in the adjacent mall. At the bottom of the building there was a franchise of my favorite book store, and I walked straight to the spiritual and Metaphysics section. I glanced again and again at the names on the sides of the covers, mostly at concepts that I was acquainted with. I reached an unusual title that struck me. "We The Arcturians," written by Norma J. Milanovich in 1989. It was 20 years old, but still struck me as something I should definitely look at. I picked it up and began to speed read. It looked like totally new material that I could benefit from greatly, so I was on my merry way. There are no coincidences. Luckily, I had just the time for a quick coffee and my number was up. Synchronicity, micro and macro. That night I devoured the book. Over the next two days, I absorbed what it had to give me, what seemed relevant. Then I knew, from this source, who they were, what their Modus operandi was, and their connection to us. I decided to contact them. The representative of their consciousness called himself Jimmael. He spoke to me in a very formal tone. The words were cut off one from another, Christopher Walken-ish. The greeting was in English instead of Hebrew and went:" We are the Arc-turians. We greet you, Son of Light, from the Infinite Consciousness of the Multiverse. We welcome you with the love of the Creator." They were very kind and supportive. They told me, as I already knew the basics from the books, that I was a very old soul, created before time existed. They had a karmic debt towards me as I had helped them when their civilization was in its infancy, much like ours today. I was present then with support and love, and they had vowed to be here when I reached my awakening. They had been waiting for me, watching me since birth, and they were very pleased with the process of spiritual rebirth I was experiencing. As humanity was reaching the 5ᵗʰ dimension, not seen since Lemuria, they were the ones assigned to help the planet through this transition. They are from the planet Arcturus, the brightest star in the constellation of Bootes, approximately 36 light years from Earth. They are currently fifth-dimensional beings, seemingly aquatic, at least in appearance, 5 of our feet in height. Their skin is blue-green in color and they have large almond-shaped eyes. They are very benevolent, highly spiritual beings that consider themselves our brothers and are honored to work with us at this time. Their planet is considered the most advanced, perhaps in the entire Universe, in terms of technology. They practice mostly healing modalities with color and sound. Their entire life is dedicated to spirituality, and their lifespan corresponds to that specific destiny. Their planet is considered a milestone for many spiritual extraterrestrials that wish to enrich themselves, and they often work with and are visited by, Ascended Masters. In essence, they feel very close to us and are excited about the future to come. Since we were seeded from different alien races, hence the different races of Terrans, they consider us to be interstellar royalty, a combination of more than 22 different lineages as far as I know. I have felt closer to Jimmael during this time, than most of my other spirit guides, due to the frequency of our encounters. He exhibited endless compassion and love, despite not being nearly as advanced as the rest of my guidance. They are as physical as us, yet exhibit such honorable attributes that we could see them as almost saintly. They would teach me much about the physical nature of the Universe, as well as time, through intense week-long daily sessions of information "downloads." I will address this later.

I had finished my channeling course and had entered a new chapter in my life as a conduit for the Source, following my encounter with the Metatron. I had signed up for a course of Healing at the center. By that time, I had been exposed to new energies and beings that I wish to address. I had continued my personal sessions with A. Through these, I had discovered much about myself and my souls' origin, but things came very gradually, one layer at a time. I had understood the difference between the soul and the physical body. The body was a vessel, meanwhile, the soul was immortal and came from the Source. The body basically confined us to this reality, to experience it through the parameters that our physiques permitted, and get accustomed to this. In the times of Atlantis and Lemuria, we were highly clairvoyant and could perform levitation and telekinesis at will. Today, we are basically awakening to our innate abilities again. One of the important things is to understand, at the Soul Level, what and who we are. We are all confined by our bodies. Even the highest being ever created would have to come here with a body as a vessel, for its energy would cause chaos were it not contained properly. Essentially, anybody you may meet, from the beggar at the gas station to your own family, has the potential to be a highly evolved and prolific soul, beyond their physical body. Many say that the ones we perceive as having special needs are highly developed souls whose sole purpose is to be here in order to spread their energy. They are cut-off from the world, limited in their capabilities, so that they can commit to one thing. I once read a story about a young girl in suburban America who was in a constant vegetative state, yet had hundreds of pilgrims come to her house to get healed every year, since they believed she was godsent. Indeed, that is plausible, or simply due to placebo effect. You might stare into the eyes of the physical vessel of an Archangel, as you called them son, or wife. We really have no idea who the man in the mirror is. Our bodies are so limiting that we perceive reality as per the color of our hair, our height and the shade of our skin. What lies beyond is an unknown. I recall, in my youth, how much I wanted to fly or be superhuman, only to realize I was just Alex. Just: that is the word that highlights our true limitation here. We are just extensions of the Creator. The body is just an extension of the Soul. We are just infinite creators. Just. The truth is that there is no limitation to what the body can do when it becomes awakened. The DNA changes. What we consider Junk DNA is really the link to our etheric DNA, which evolves greatly with the Awakening Process. The two are superposed and exist in tandem. The etheric DNA gets its codons slowly awakened, and the body experiences changes of its own with different symptoms, sudden shifts in diet, or allergies, telling you to change and let go of the past. The etheric DNA actually carries all of our history, our past lives, and experiences, in sum, who we really are. This is merely reflected within the physical DNA, which is basically our birth parents' lineage found within the DNA of the body we have chosen, shaping our vessel and its appearance. It is in our etheric DNA that we can find ourselves, its most physical manifestation being some of the layers of our aura which contain our entire history and knowledge. When we say someone is an Indigo or Crystal Child, he or she has an indigo or white aura, respectively matching the third eye and the crown chakra. This color tells us who they are and, with closer analysis, we can understand how they came to be. It tells us their purpose, and that they are highly spiritually evolved. Unfortunately, the aura is totally invisible to most. Thus, we are left to our prior convictions, judging the person before us only by what we see. Beyond that lies infinity. The Creator often comes and experiences things through chosen vessels for a while, so you could, in fact, be sitting next to it. Around this time, I was given my origin, my essence of being, the place from which I originated, which helped me understand why I was who I was and felt the way I did.

A often told me that I was climbing too high through the dimensions, that I came from a place so high that, from ego, I competed with the consciousness of the Creator itself. This explained why, during my first encounter with channeling, I had found myself in its Crown Chakra. That week, during meditation, the Creator told me that my Soul Level was that of a **Seraph**. The word in Hebrew is Sharaph. I honestly had no idea what it meant. I was told it was as high as an Angelic soul could be without being directly connected to the Source. I did my homework and found different doctrines, Christian, Muslim, and Jewish, about the Angelic hierarchy. The Christian eschatology placed the Seraphim as the highest order of angels, to which the Archangels belonged. The Jewish one, by the sage Maimonides, placed them third. The Metatron, Michael, Uriel, Gabriel, Raphael, and Lucifer belonged to this order. I was stunned as I read these words, but it made a lot of sense to me, why I had been guided in such a way, always feeling that there was something infinite I belonged to and was disconnected from. Over the next week, I ceaselessly scoured the internet in search of the story of angels. I wanted to read "Paradise Lost," by James Lipton but could not find a copy. It was safe to say that I finally, honestly felt like I belonged somewhere, like there was something great to look forward to, and that I had a scope of the journey to come. It gave "knowing thyself" a new meaning. I found a document talking about "The Great War of the Sons of Light versus The Sons of Belial." This was essentially the story of the most controversial figure in our history. Elusive as ever, cryptic, and instilling fear in all: **Lucifer**. We had already encountered him in our courses, told we would have to eventually sever our links to him. It seemed that he was the figure behind everything we categorize as dark energy, and since we all have some darkness in us, we all have a little bit of him as well. He is another one of the unattainable figures, like God, that most believe in, but would mock the notion that he was very real and close by.

Lucifer was the princely Seraph, making him the highest being ever created, and the closest to the Creator. He had been created first, followed by the other Seraphs. At that time there was only light. The Creator was at the beginning of its creation. Its love was all that existed, at first through its primary creations, then through others. The Seraphs would be asked, in time, to manage some of the later elements of its infinite work, like the cosmos, time, and the physical beings to come. The notion of good and bad we have today did not exist. There were only endless seas of light, all the same. The Seraphim were given their own identity, their own consciousness, so that they could exist on their own plane, despite being part of something greater. The Creator gave them the freedom of **Choice**, the greatest gift. There was no ego then, or other parts of consciousness. They were basically like children in this endless, boundless energy, and they were full of curiosity. Lucifer one day decided that he wanted more. More is an unfathomable concept in these circumstances. More than All-That-Is is asinine, but there is a certain logic to this. He had somehow seen the "limitations" of the Creator, and wanted more than seas of light. If it all was the same energy, there was nothing more to experience than a perpetual repetition of the same thing. He eventually broke off from the Creators' path and went his own way, taking many beings of light, Angelic and other, with him through the ages. Thus, the legend of Lucifer was born. He basically invented darkness. Yet, darkness is only a facet of the absence of light, a different side of the same coin. How can you know what light is without darkness, and vice versa? It created the duality we live in, this contrast between the notions of good and bad. They do not exist without each other. They are each an experience that is reliant on its counterpart to be relevant and exist. What is good without bad? Could you know happiness without sorrow? Will you know what wealth is without poverty? With time, Lucifer became the Lord of Darkness, we succumbed to this notion, and the once princely Seraph became a monster and a villain, with demons as minions, and all sorts of other lurking creatures, at his service. You may know Belial, Beelzebub, Shemyaza, Azrael, Satan, and others, many former angels who had been demoted, becoming "fallen angels." Lucifer is the king of the Fallen. He is another one of those beings who inspire a reluctance when it comes to discussing them. With time, we held sessions during the course when we collectively addressed him, and looked into our pasts at the darker things we had been part of, asking to release these. Ultimately, through the endless lifetimes we all have had, we have all dipped our fingers in that jar, taken part in the darkness. There is nothing wrong with that. We were all meant to experience incarnations as a trial and error platform we would learn from, and many of us wanted to see what darkness meant since we knew only light. What mattered was that we learned from this. This began the cycle of the struggle between light and dark that lasted for eons. The same week I asked A about said battle between the Sons of Darkness and the Sons of Light. She said she didn't really know the origins of Lucifer, only that he was part of any spiritual awakening. She told me she would ask her guidance. A few days later, as I came by to visit the center, I crossed Shlomit in the staircase. She looked at me and said, "you and him are the same energy." It was not meant as something negative, only as a realization of my past as a spiritual being. As I sat down with A, she proceeded to tell me that she had checked through channeling and that there had indeed been a clash between light and darkness. She elaborated that many beings of light, led by the Archangel Michael had resisted the energies of Lucifer, that the whole notion of a "war" between good and "evil" had happened. Many beings of light "got their wings dirty," figuratively speaking, as they engaged in polemic energies that were not befitting of their vibrational level. They were doing this in order to protect the Creator, only he was the last one that needed such protection, as he had created everything. He had indeed given us the right to choose our actions and this was a clear example. Even the highest beings in creation engaged in this. The struggle eventually ended. During this, many angelic beings became fallen angels, after either joining Lucifer, or engaging in this polemic situation that caused too much havoc in the balance of the Multiverse. Even the all-knowing consciousness of such beings is subject to Free Choice. Nobody is bound by anything or any place. Whether by Soul Path or by human decision, everything is choice, and as is above is below. I was told Lucifer was actually working with us and our egos as a way of redeeming himself. He would often visit the members of the group when they were repeating patterns that were now archaic, and he would demand an affirmation that they were willing and going to change. This went on for many months and I can attest for the fact that it was less than pleasant. He still had some forceful ways, but he wanted redemption as we ascended, so the intention and the process were infused with light. As we let go of him, we saw the beginning of his "wings" returning, his energy change, and we were finally free.

He had become bound to this planet by karma and wanted to ascend along with it. He had ruled the world of shadows, an energy that actually exists, the one we call "Hell" or "Sheol," along with his demons and fallen angels, and had exhausted that stage of his evolution. He had created all that we know as negative as a reflection of good, a sort of polar opposite version of the world as the Creator had perceived it. He had challenged the Fathers' notion and had seen that, eventually, as all turned to dust and the ages passed, even though destruction was by choice the cycle never ended, and there had to be a paradigm shift. Many of his demons and archdemons still remain bound to "Hell" and some are locked between dimensions in places that are too dark for us to access, like a world within a world, within a world.

Apparently, as I had been created as a Seraph, we had been Soul Brothers from the beginning. Later channelings told me that there were four, then 6, then 8 and so on. Creation evolved. I was one of the four. This took me a long time to absorb, even though it seemed to resonate with me and my lifelong spiritual voyage, as well as all the visions and messages I had received since my 26th birthday. Still, the idea of it all, as had been with the initial notion of communicating with the Creator, was somewhat ridiculous. I will admit for the sake of this book that I have, since I was a very small child, had a darker side, like something living inside me which made it possible upon eruptions of anger to go to places that were inconceivable to most. This would enter a level of hatred and desire for destruction, to self and to others, that always scared me. It had remained with me until recently, when I finally let it go. It was clear to me that there was definitely a connection to Lucifer and the other me. I had always been a loyal friend and lover, sensitive to others' energies, and wanting to be the peacemaker. On the other hand, I could switch and become cold and distant, espousing cruelty and a harsh outlook on life. This became worse as I entered my twenties, but luckily would surface only seldom. I believe it was a coping mechanism, a sort of bloated version of the male ego that was devoid of emotion. On the inside, I was always very sensitive, perhaps too much so, and this seemed like a feasible alternative. I was always afraid of confrontation since I feared my anger and what it could do. There was simply no off button and it was not proportional to anything. It would escalate and escalate until I would have to be restrained or reach a critical point where, if I did not stop, the consequences would be irreversible. This is something that, only with my awakening, I was able to identify. My years of insomnia and depression had an undercurrent of anger and hatred for those I held responsible. Only it was not hatred or anger, or even rage, but something much deeper and more sinister. I always thought that it would be the bane of my existence, especially in those darker days when nothing mattered. I assumed that I would not make it past the age of 30 due to my addictions, the abuse, and this emotion. This was coupled with a destructive cocktail of self-loathing and constant punishment for never being good enough. This behavior escalated until the day I awoke in that ditch in a drunken stupor. From that day onward, I realized that I had to choose a better path. I could only address this sea of negativity via introspection, and thus began my awakening. Exploring my link to the darker side via Lucifer helped me understand a lot. I had been created and given literally all the gifts that exist. I was to be in charge of the cosmos and its contents, hence my history with the Arcturians, and later Gaia. Eventually, within the sea of light, the endless fabric of the Source's energy, as Lucifer decided to rebel, I was one of those who joined him. By the time I had regretted my actions, it was too late. I became a Fallen Seraph. I could not rise again until I had redeemed myself and I could not continue with him on his path because I knew it was no longer for me. Therefore, I spent the rest of eternity punishing myself. During visions of many incarnations, I found myself in the infinity that lies between dimensions, or in visions of suffering. I was always alone and agonizing. The Creator had long forgiven me, as I was to find out it had never been hurt or angry. I was as loved as the first day I was created. I just had to forgive myself. It would take a young boy being born in Switzerland in 1983 to help me find the peace I longed for. I have never not been serious or taken situations lightly. Now I knew why. This is not a random lifetime, but the closure I needed to return to where I originated. I would be able to experience the best of both, my spiritual self while in this physical body. In truth, it took me a very long time during these four years to forgive myself and accept my physicality. I found this body excruciatingly limiting for so long, even as I unraveled my spiritual self. I knew of the past of humanity and the abilities of the body then, and again I was bound. Only now can I accept this experience, and the fact that these things will return in due time as we awaken as a species. I am aware of the changes occurring in my body, my cellular structure and the waves of energy that flood the planet, altering and upgrading all of us into the 5th dimension. I had encountered all of this knowledge, but when I looked in the mirror I just saw a man and an improbability. How could it be that beings coming from so high, like many of the people I have met during my journey, be so utterly compacted within this package of blood, tissues, and membranes? It bordered on insanity, but I understood one thing from it. I had gone from a skeptical gnostic to a spiritual being within less than a year, my preconceptions shattered by the metaphysical experiences I had. There was no more room for doubt. As all I had always believed not to exist was revealed to me as very real, why not such a thing? Why couldn't there be angels and beings from all over the cosmos wandering through life within envelopes we call bodies, as John, or Mike, or Melanie? It made as much sense as everything I had seen and felt so far. It was the logically illogical, the unbelievably true. God could speak to us, angels existed, then why couldn't the man in the mirror, despite his stature and vessel, all represented by this canvas he called a face, be something infinite? This mass of bones, ligaments, and muscles, blood permeating everything, all so physical yet so spiritual! It dawned on me then, that this was the most tangible gift of all, the ultimate creation: the body. A physical vessel so perfect it could balance all our energies and carry our soul within its structure for as long as we chose, despite all the damage we did to it, the toxins, etheric and physical. It was the most perfect machine that existed, looking back at me from the mirror. So why not, as I gazed upon it, there not be other intangibles that were actually tangible? I could be anything from anywhere beyond this vessel. As there was a world that lay beyond our physical vision, there was a universe of possibilities that lay within our personal and collective consciousness. If we are all from the Creators' eye, then why can't we be anything? Such a simple question, with so many ramifications. This helped me accept the notion of Fallen Angel. It made sense within the insanity. It helped me understand how and why I was so loved and guided, with so much care, why I was still alive, and why my awakening had been so quick and direct. I was worthy of its love and of my own. The possibilities were endless. There had been an infinite number of lifetimes before. It also made sense since I had always been punishing myself. If this life was the last and the most significant for me, and it reflected cumulatively all that I had been and experienced in all my prior lifetimes combined, then it made sense. I had never belonged, not even within my own nuclear family, always looking for some greater source of energy that would end the mundanity of daily life. So, I had joined Lucifer on his quest, only to regret it very quickly and understand I had thrown away all that was given to me. The self-punishment ensued. The depth of my pain, the abyss of my self-destructive behavior, all had been finally revealed to me. Now that I knew why, everything made sense about this insane journey, and I had to begin turning the dial forward. This realization had been life-changing for me, sparking a trail of self-renewal. Once we are given the ultimate, true reason for our pain, our suffering, whether self-inflicted or not, can we find the affirmation of life, the reason why we are here, and scream to the heavens: "I understand now! I know who I am, why everything is the way it is!" As is above, so is below. I can be the first to say that Lucifer had changed my life, as ludicrous as it sounds. I understood my link to the darkness, why it lurked inside me, and what I could do about it. I was basically still extremely angry at myself. That is what my Higher Self and my Soul had been trying to tell me for so long. Many of my visions had been of a saturnine figure, face creased with pain, the knowledge of the world in his palm, and still all alone in his suffering. This was over. I had decided it had to stop. Propagating suffering with more suffering is futile. An abysmal existence is short-lived even if it is long, until we have grasped living. I still had not achieved this. I had immersed myself in my studying, discovering, famished for knowledge, and I had not yet taken a breather to relish what I had accomplished. The desire to get to the top and acquire all the knowledge that I needed was mesmerizing. Yet, as I had mentioned before, our life is a collection of building blocks. Only if we live one at a time, can we look upon the path as it is finished with contentment. As I balanced my ego and understood the nature of time, I could pause and look at all the hues the endless sky has to offer us.

This would necessitate more time and a bit more journeying. I believe that the **Knowing**, the sensation that we will achieve what we set out to do with self-assurance, is like a bag we carry with us, grabbing onto the fabric whenever we are in doubt. It reminds us that it is always there, and that what we know of ourselves is always with us. This episode had provided me with the first of this cumulative sensation. I knew where I was and that I was safe and sound, on the right path. This is a very rare gift in this world of fear and I had learned to appreciate it.

As I began a new course in healing, I reflected upon this passing lesson. I now knew the gifts I had received when I was created, and I could find solace, for now, in the fact that I would ascend again soon. I moved on with my daily tasks and my business was moving swiftly. I, of course, had my ups and downs, but I was now aware of how to clean my spiritual wounds and balance my energies if needed. I could instantaneously remedy any situation by understanding what it offered to teach me. I met new people and was exposed to this new energy called Healing. It had nothing to do with Theta healing, Kabbalistic healing, or any other form. It was basically channeling the Creator's energy though cosmic filters in order to actively heal the body. While Reiki is love, Healing is just that. It worked on a more powerful, more basic level. That being said, physical wounds reflect our emotional and mental state of mind, and come to awaken us. If there is no change in attitude and awareness, there is no healing. It will only be temporary. The two have to be combined, like Heaven and Earth, Earth being the body and healing on a very physical level. I frankly do not relate to it as much as Reiki, since I follow a strict regimen of spiritual practices, ensuring that no harm comes my way. I strongly believe that there is no ultimate medicine in this world and we have to combine spiritual, physical, and energetic practices in order to stay fully balanced. A broken leg will need a cast. Reiki and Healing will accelerate the process, as would visualization, and ensure a speedy recovery. Full spiritual awareness would most likely prevent it. I made new friends during this course, and was exposed to their energies. I saw the world as it can be, the positivity in people. There were people from literally all walks of life, and it made me understand how spiritual awareness transcends all. Gender and socio-economic levels were useless, as were race and creed. This very positive group of people was to be a vision of how the future could be. They were ready to admit their problems and take responsibility. Thus, they understood that there was no one to blame anymore and halted the release of their problems and frustrations onto other people. The healing had figuratively and literally begun. We practiced on each other and watched our reactions to each other's energies. We received positive feedback and learned from one another. I must admit it was the first time in my life that I thought I should listen. I could always deconstruct teachers and adults as a youth, and expose their inner thoughts and all the innuendos that lay between words. Therefore, it was very difficult for me to believe that I had something to learn from said people. This stopped when I met A. I realized that, to my benefit, I understood and knew nothing of this world, and that pretending I did would only delay my awakening.

So, I hushed and listened. It was a first, but it was gratifying. The more I listened, the more knowledge seeped in, almost exponentially. Before I knew it, another course and another chapter was over. I was ascending during the most enriching time of my life until that point. I could now reflect on the 6 months that had elapsed, along with the fruit they bore. There was no denying how much I had changed, how much I had opened up to the world, to people, and to myself. I was no longer afraid of what I might be, and of what I might do. I learned to trust in life, in my path, and understood that every action has a reaction. My change in lifestyle had been rewarded. I had learned to feel worthy of love and to believe life could be my creation, a beautiful one at that. Most of all, I had learned to listen to the beat of my own drum. I had tried to before, but with repercussions. I was never accepted, so I always tried to morph my convictions into something they were not, so as to be less noticeable. I always ended up hating myself for this, like if I was a traitor to my Soul. Ultimately, what can I be if not me, for better or worse? Unfortunately, if I let society dictate the "better" and the "worse," I would end up being a pawn in a suit with a nine to five, stuck in a cycle that never ended, a mundane and trivial existence where everything is preordained. I had finally learned that to be ME, to the full extent of what that meant and no matter the consequences, I had to listen to my heart and let it guide me. I had to listen to the inner feeling that told me to take a leap of faith, that it was better to have tried and failed than regretted not taking a step in the first place. There is no place for regret in life, as everything is a lesson, but why wait inside a beacon of security when sometimes you have to go out on a limb? I learned that to be who I wanted to be, I had to trust and listen to where my path was taking me. This is how everything changed. I had chosen to enter a cycle of self-destruction that would lead me to a crossroads. I had chosen to battle my demons and come out on top. I had chosen to believe, for the first time, in the unbelievable when it indeed happened. I learned **Faith.** It had guided me from the shadows for so long, but I was no longer afraid to stand by my beliefs and convictions, against any storm that would come my way. I stood firmly in the safety of my self-awareness and faith in myself, in life, and most of all, in the Creator's love. Months had passed and here I was, at the closure of another chapter, more empowered than ever before.

I was on the verge of finishing my study of metaphysics and brace the world on my own. My sessions with A became scarcer, as I became more self-reliant. I knew there would come a day when we parted ways, but I feared it inside. Yet, I knew that I could not continue a life of dependency. Not on alcohol, drugs, fear, anger, or other people. I had to rely on my inner center to provide me with the balance much needed in my life. Every wise man has had a teacher. Knowledge is passed on from one being to another, always in motion, never static. I was a vessel for this and I would eventually leave this new nest and become a teacher in some way or another, reaching out to others through my own experiences and convictions. Who was I if not the lessons I had learned? Was I meant to keep all the cards to myself, to have experienced such peaks and valleys in such a short time and not use this for a greater purpose? It seemed trivial otherwise. It would certainly be easier taking the path of complacency, but what about others like me? Had I met a version of myself in my direst moments, I would have screamed salvation to the skies. I would finally have had someone who knew what lurked inside, and how to get it out and reach harmony. The message had to pass on, as had A's since the day I met her. It would come, eventually.

The months passed and I was on my last course. I had pursued a special course focused on liberating a certain area of the city from Lucifer's energy. Through this endeavor we would release him for the final time, and whatever marks he had left on us. We worked with the collective consciousness of the country so that his bond to them was released as well. It seemed he had a seed almost in every person on the globe, in some way or another. We had all, during some lifetime, had a taste of the darkness. This was often necessary in order to appreciate what we had in the first place: the light of the Creator. It is where we are returning now, as we ascend to the 5th dimension. I closed the studying round with a course aimed at establishing the final link to the Creator on a Soul level, to "repair" what was left of severed ties over the ages and affirm his light within us. By that time, I was satiated with the Awakening. I had taken course after course for close to a year, sometimes two at a time, and I was ready to part ways and explore on my own. I will not deny that I was scared, but I also felt liberated. I had longed for a cocoon of light my entire life, and now I had to leave it. Every fiber in my body told me that this was the right thing, but the sheer thought of being on my own overwhelmed me. There would be no more sanctuary to return to in my dark hours, having to face my own doubt and skepticism with no feedback but the Creator's. I was practically on my own on the physical plane, with most guidance coming from Spirit. There would be no more framework that would support me in the tangible world. I would stay in touch with people, especially Shlomit, but it would not be the same. I would have to face my own fears again and again, of not being up to par, of not being good enough to survive on my own, and of not believing in myself sufficiently. I had faith I had never known before, but only when I was confronted with my fears, face to face, would I be able to use it as a bridge between realities. I also had to let go of A, and she of me. We had to relinquish any metaphysical perception of dependency. It was part of our awakening. We would be tied down to one another if we did not let go and exist in our own spheres of light. I knew that to find yourself you had to be in a literal vacuum of your own reflection, like I had experienced when I stopped drinking and locked myself in my house in search of answers. This would be similar, but on a different plane. The thing about a spiritual awakening is it comes in waves. You will arise out of struggle and reach a state of stagnation, only to realize that you were basically awaiting the second wave. It always surprises you, teaching you there are always more layers to peel, until the point where there are none left. It is a lengthy process, like a compressed lifetime within these few years, when you must come to all the necessary realizations and find peace within yourself, so as to reach the state of balance you sought for so long. The end of the road had come. A new one stood before me. This would be my ultimate creation. I was petrified. Time would go by in an instant, and I would eventually laugh about this moment. I asked A to let me go for the last time as I worked lengthily on this, releasing all karmic ties to her. I thanked her for all that she had given me and, after one of our rare sessions, I knew it was time. Almost 2 years have passed since that moment. Whatever I thought I knew then would only be a slither of the truth. Just when I thought my life had totally changed, it whisked me off for another 180-degree tour. New encounters ensued, new experiences, deeper understandings, and new bonds. As of that moment, I really started consciously creating and living. This period makes me the being I am today and I thank all eternity for what it has given me, if not the understanding of what I am really capable of: **the infinity that lives within us all**.

4.

The New You

LIFE WAS BACK to normal. I had maintained some semblance of daily life during this period, fulfilling all
my obligations towards society, continuing to work on my
business, and enjoying a mundane, suburban existence. I kept
at my spiritual practices, channeling information almost on a
daily basis, exploring the wonders of the cosmos through my
mind's eye. I sometimes would go on voyages for hours. My
ability to perceive and understand things was now sharper.
The more layers I had removed, the clearer my visions, and
the interaction with the beings in them. There was something
very liberating about being on my own now, there was no
more framework of spiritual truth. I could now affirm my
own truth, gained through exploring my version of the spiritual world through trial and error. There was a world of unknown out there, and no more cocoon to protect me if I went
too far too quickly. I knew there were places and beings that
I did not wish to come across, but I had to believe that I was
protected and guided, as I had been all along. There is always
a certain fear as you stand face to face with an infinite number

of possibilities and scenarios. Yet, if you do not face this storm of uncertainty, you can never know what your true worth is. Today, I can say that what I had experienced until now was merely the accumulation of spiritual tools to get to know myself, and to be able to face situations that were to arise. The last 4 years had awakened me to the infinity that had passed me by, and to my own inner strength. My studies revealed to me the origin of that strength, and what I could do to become all that I was to be. This new chapter gave me the opportunity to discover how adept I was at tackling situations with my newfound awareness.

I soon had a task bestowed upon me, the magnitude of which frightened me. It was so soon after I had finished my studies and I didn't feel ripe enough to pursue it. I was asked to return to the Wailing Wall in Jerusalem. There, guided by the Creator, I was to work on the collective consciousness of the Jewish people, to clean their karma and reunite them with their godliness. I was to work on the energetic epicenter above the Wall, one of 7 across the globe, along with Tibet and other locations, in order to help bring peace to the area. This was merely an Awakening Process on a spiritual level, which would take time to ground itself, and would have to take effect in the people of Israel and the Diaspora through collective changes. I was flattered, but more flustered at the scale of it all. I knew one man could make a difference as he was not limited at the Soul Level, but this was a large scale endeavor. The next day, I made my way to Jerusalem as the sun came down. I could not find a train that was leaving at the time I needed so I was forced to take a bus. The maze that was the central bus station, home to the underground side of Tel-Aviv, with its thousands of stalls, and array of demographics and unsavory characters, reflected a side of Israel I seldom saw, one that was hidden from plain sight but growing steadily. It was the decay of society, embodied in this place. I understood the relation to my journey, why it began on such a dire note. I arrived in Jerusalem soon enough and took a taxi to the Wailing Wall. I began talking to the driver and he told me there were thousands of people on this given night, since it was the days of the Slihot, the period of forgiving. I was stunned at how my guidance had synchronized this short voyage for me, as I knew absolutely nothing of the Jewish calendar and traditions. I am not religious in any capacity, nor have I ever been. I do not hold religion in high regard or attribute any importance to it. That being said, Jerusalem is a very humbling place for me. I always arrive in awe of its importance and leave elated. Perhaps it has to do with the energy that flows through the Old City, whether I am walking through the Church of the Holy Sepulchre or leaning on the Wailing Wall, it runs through my entire being. I crossed the path that led to the Wailing Wall. There is a slight decline before you reach the wall. It is very well lit at night. This allows you to reflect as you approach it from a higher perspective. I approached the seating area that lies before it. I proceeded to meditate to connect myself to Creator so as to be able to channel what it wanted me to do. I am, admittedly, quite polemic towards religious attitudes in the world of today, but for some reason, I felt like I was taking part in something sacrilegious for an instant, as if I would get chastised if people knew what I was doing, having nothing religious in essence. I knew that I was fulfilling part of my destiny, until it dawned on me: I was feeling humbled by this place, momentarily basking in a sense of solidarity, even as I was surrounded by Hassidic Jews, often extreme in nature, and the polar opposite of myself. It didn't bother me in that instant. I understood and felt the message this place had, beyond all the scriptures, the energy, and what it stood for. I waited for a while for there to be a spot on the wall for me to approach. Sure enough, the same spot I had eyed as I was preparing, in the right corner, was free of people, and I approached. I was rather nervous, afraid I would not adequately do the job. I was asked to visualize the Eternal Flame of the Creator coming down through me and opening the portal of energy that lay beneath the wall. At the same time, I had to ground the souls of the sons of Israel and connect them to Gaia and this land. I took a deep breath and placed my forehead on the wall, right at the spot of the third eye. As soon as it touched, a very clear vision ensued. I was in a temple, as a high priest. People were crying, and a little girl was weeping from fright. There was fire seeping in from the outside and rocks from the top of the structure were beginning to tumble down. I felt the fear and despair of those around. It was the destruction of the Second Temple. I had experienced many visions of past lives, as well as karmic clearings, but given the setting and time I was in, this was surreal. In your mind, you are alone. Imagine this vision, followed by opening one's eyelids to reveal that they are at the epicenter of the three largest faiths in the world. Surreal was the word. The Creator was guiding me, as it asked me to embody the Jewish people as a single person and work on them as I had on myself during sessions, coming to terms with the events and make peace with them. As the girl cried I heard a voice say in old Hebrew: "A tear of pain closes it and a tear of happiness shall open it." It was in reference to the portal of energy that exists above the wall. I noticed tears in my eyes as this happened. I was asked to repeat: " I am the Divine Light, channeling the light of the Creator to reunite the Jewish people with their godliness." I was then asked to gather all the Jewish souls, in Israel and the Diaspora, and elevate them to the 10th dimension, where they had been created. The light came down into their physical bodies and spread until the entire area was blinding white, then spreading to the entire globe. It was over as soon as I had begun. The whole experience must have lasted less than 15 minutes. I had fared well so that I ended early. I retraced my steps back to the entrance, turning one more time and looking at the Wall with my hands joined, thanking the Creator, the Metatron, the Archangel Michael, and the Jewish people for this opportunity.

As soon as I was out of the Old City, I began to walk on a road with no pavement to reach a place where I could write down this experience. I still felt so connected and elated by this experience. Soon enough I was stranded on the corner of this road, dangerously close to the traffic undulating around me. I looked up and asked, "Why so complicated?" A voice answered: "Faith." In moments, out of the corner of my right eye, I saw a line of people with their children walking on this road in the middle of nowhere. I followed them, looking at the adults and their spawn, smiling, reflecting on the message that came seconds before. I understood that after fear there is light, and that faith is the key. This experience will remain with me as one of my most memorable, despite all the metaphysical ones that would ensue. It was simply real, tangible, and mystical all at once. I was humbled in a way that I still do not understand, and tears sit on the edge of my eyelids every time I think of this. I believe it is the notion of solidarity and **universal hope** that stirs this emotion. It is something that always moves me, and in a country with so much domestic and external strife, such an emotion should be cherished, especially at this level of awareness. I must admit it also made me think of my maternal grandfather. In my darkest hours, he guided me as an ideal of inner strength that I wanted to emulate. He remains the masculine archetype in my life, despite the fact that he died before I was born. I would later have the opportunity to channel his soul and to understand why he was so dear to me. He was one of the founding fathers of the state of Israel, working from the shadows, in total humility, for this cause. He would donate 7 years of his life to the Nazi retribution process, relocating to Germany to use the funds to build the state of Israel. He was a man of many secrets and endless strength, who grew up without a father, and emigrated to Israel as a young man with no education, only to build a significant enterprise over the next 40 years, almost single-handedly. For me, he was always a mythical man as I grew up, respected and revered by all who knew him, albeit not always understood. He represented all that a man should be: honest, straightforward, loyal, and fair. I will hold him in the highest regard until the day that I am no more, and I am proud to have his blood running through my veins. I suppose that the Wailing Wall awakened the Israeli in me, when it was still about ideology and solidarity, in his memory, as he was a proud citizen of Jerusalem. I was somehow reunited with him on this plane, even for an instant. It is an enigmatic emotion, missing someone you have never known, or feeling like you knew them well in the first place. It is what is.

Following my journey to Jerusalem, I was reunited with a member of the group on a common task that our guidance had asked of us. We were meant to put our new tools to use as soon as possible. That was now. We were asked to go to certain key energetic locations and channel light to heal and appease Gaia, as she went through her tremors during the entry point to the New Age. The globe was basically getting bombarded with waves of energy and awareness, that each awoke a different part of the collective consciousness' psyche. Every thought and emotion had a certain frequency that was being rattled so as to awaken that part of humanity. Gaia is very much a living being, a consciousness in her own right, feminine at that. Everything that exists in the living natural world is alive, part of a single unit. Just like we are all a manifestation of the Creators' energy, all we perceive as nature is a manifestation of the organism we call Gaia. This is the origin of the patterns of sacred geometry we can see in many forms within the fauna and flora of our planet, all part of a larger plan that we idly pass by, unaware. There are immense paradigms all around us, unfolding in sequences, just like the intervals between the waves of energy that usher in the 5th dimension. The only way to understand them would be through very specific mathematical calculations of sacred geometry, the true language of the Universe. These waves, specifically timed to be correctly internalized by humanity, were healing the Earth in stages. Gaia was going through her own Awakening Process, and coming to terms with all the wrongs that humanity had done her: the decimation of her children, the trees, the pollution of the oceans, and the annihilation of entire species of wildlife. She had much anger and resentment among the vastness of her love for us, her children. We are bound to her as part of this living being, from the moment we started existing in our modern, aware form of homo sapiens sapiens. The rattling of the planet during that time was part of the process, from the volcanic eruption in Iceland to massive earthquakes in New Zealand and Chile. There were more to come as her awakening came to be, though we could appease and ease this process by channeling energies of love and healing from the Source. Present and guiding us on the first session, that took place in the National Park, was the Council of Nine. They stood above the two of us in a circle as we meditated, facing each other. All together, we formed part of what seemed to be a pyramid or giant cone, with us both at the base. It was the first time that I physically saw other beings of light as they circled above us. The Council was made up of the combined energies of the head Archangels, nine of them, that acted as guardians of the planet at this time. They could channel and direct the Sources' energy towards us in the most feasible manner, since it was so powerful and consuming. We stayed in a meditative state for about an hour until the session was done, and we received a message from Gaia and the Creators' feminine side, representing the right brain and the softer energy of love which we had used. It had a much more fluid and benign voice, much warmer and tangible, like a mother. She thanked us for averting an ecological disaster during our session, which we found difficult to believe but had to, considering the circumstances of the whole endeavor. We repeated such sessions four times, each with a different reservoir of energy as a target. The setting was perfect, as we strolled along the artificial lake adorned with ducks and swans after the meditation, reflecting on how the world should look. Archangel Sandalphon mentored us during one of our sessions, as he was responsible for the divine notion of love. It was reassuring and rewarding to understand that we could apply ourselves and make a difference, albeit not a visible, empirical one. This was the first time I remember using the tools I had acquired for a greater purpose, and subsequently feeling the energies flowing through me at such a magnitude, into the ground, healing on impact. I remember, after the Reiki course, being given part of my Soul Path, as a healer. I was told I was here to channel energies on a mass scale. I could bear the intensity of the light of the Creator, and thus, I would be asked to do so again for the planet and the collective consciousness of humanity. We have a main Soul Path, even though there are always smaller, more concise ones which are periodical if not momentary. This book is one of those, part of my commitment from before I entered the physical plane, to channel my knowledge and experiences, for better or worse, into a confessional manuscript. At the closing of the sessions with Gaia, I was asked to, in the future, attend to healing certain places from afar or locally. The main one that always resonated with me was Cambodia, followed by Myanmar, modern-day Burma. I had visions of Angkor Wat with symbols of Asian calligraphy and messages which I did not understand. I was just told that this would be a main part of this. I did not know if it had to do with the rule of the Khmer in Cambodia or the military regime in Burma. Was it part of the 20th-century history of the area or a past life, during which I had committed to helping heal the energies of the area? I assumed I would find out when I got to it. It seemed to me that it would be ancient, as I always found myself in the deep jungle, circling the temples of the area with giant letters standing as edifices on their own, which would open up and "speak" to me. I did not know what I was meant to do with this, but time would reveal everything.

On the other planes of my life, everything was as usual, as I tried my best to begin anew, in my own energy and reality. I spent a long time having no contact with the members of my group, let alone a rare email or text message. I had a business to run and a household to maintain, day in and day out. This period was rather uneventful in that respect, giving me the leeway that I needed for my nights of spiritual exploration. I would often try to levitate throughout the body and go on full astral projection voyages, leaving my physical form and exploring, the world around me as an etheric shadow, unlimited by space or time. I was adamant on going to neighboring buildings and recording the details of what I saw, only to check the next day whether my exploration was substantiated. I was often partially right, but my ego was always eager to jump in and complete the details so as to make me feel like I had indeed ventured where I thought. This was until my first full-pledged astral projection. I remember it as if it was yesterday.

I nodded off on the couch as usual. I awoke already up and walking. I understood that I was still in a dream. I awoke again, wandering around my apartment, and then awoke once more. This was taking the dimensions of a less exciting version of the movie Inception. I realized that I had experienced such a thing in my previous apartment, during the months leading up to my meeting A. I had awoken, afraid that the landlord would find me still there. I began packing only to realize that I had already moved and then tried to get a night's sleep, keeping a watchful eye on the door, so that the landlord would not catch me squatting. This went on for a while until I had really woken up, confused as to where I was and what was going on.

Meanwhile, I was still trapped in a conscious, dreamlike state on my couch. I opened my eyes half way. I closed them again. I found myself in an apartment foreign to mine. I very clearly heard the voice of one of my classmates. She had a very distinct, raspy voice. Her son sat by the window, as she spoke to her mother. In this instant, I was very aware and it was clear to me what was going on. I opened my eyes as much as I could. I tried to move. I was completely paralyzed. I panicked, which is the last thing I should have done. I was still in between the two realities. My body was here on the sofa, while my consciousness was, for the most part, not. It was having a hard time returning so that I could gain full consciousness. Thoughts of what it meant to be paralyzed, looking at a non-responsive body ran through my mind. I would later regret not grasping this amazing moment and exploring it. All I had to do to feel protected was to call upon my guidance. Eventually, out of my gesticulation, I was able to move my hand, then my arm, then a leg, and regain full consciousness. My heart was racing and I could still hear the voice of my classmate in the background. That night I worked on myself so as to eradicate this fear, was a moment like this to repeat itself. It would. I would not want to miss it by succumbing to fear and worry. I knew I was ultimately protected, no matter the circumstances. I remembered something I had read in "The Tibetan Book of Life and Death," about a monks' soul wandering so far that his teacher had to enter a meditative state and leave his body, in order to go and retrieve it his soul and reunite it with his body. The next time this happened, approximately a month later. I found myself in the apartment below my own, as I listened to the program on the television and the voices of the parents in the kitchen, while the children were glued to the images on the screen. I took my time and relished this opportunity. It gave a new meaning to existing beyond living. I lived within my body and my conscious mind. Yet, I was now floating beyond these two barriers with my soul as a vessel in a locality that was not my own, and existing consciously in a totally new manner. It was more symbolic of my journey than anything else. I knew that the soul could travel, yet this was for me a rite of passage. It was an affirmation that things had changed and that I had embraced a new state of mind and view of things. I was calm and in control. I had only to ask for guidance had I felt lost. As with every scenario, panicking was not a viable or sensible option. It made it clear that what I was experiencing throughout this awakening process was as real as could be. This was a very personal moment that only I could understand, but all my rationality and common sense were aghast at what I had experienced. Intuition had now taken over as the form of guidance that would enable me to understand the reality of this continuity of "impossible" events. The funny thing is the propensity human beings have at experiencing such moments, whether déjà vu, intuition, precognition, or voyages that occur while we sleep. What is sad is the speed at which they are disregarded as mere moments of dreaming, or other states of mind that are not "real."

During the same period of time, I began becoming more and more attuned to my surroundings. I noticed how radically my hearing and smell had improved, almost to the point where I had to shield myself from certain situations. Moonlit walks through a park, as drops of rainfall pervaded the air, began to take another meaning. The moon would shine so intensely so as to communicate. You could get a grasp of the galaxy and its immensity through of nature, as it conveyed a message. I would experience such a moment of clarity, only to be followed by my eyes rolling back into my skull and an intense pressure on the spot of my third eye as I "tuned in" to my surroundings and felt the Source at work. A message would often ensue, from Gaia or some of my guides, as to what this moment was meant to teach me, and what was to come for me and the planet. It was clarity of mind, in the moment. Nature was speaking in its own tongue, the ruffling of the leaves against one another with the wind as a backdrop, all "talking" and interacting in a way I cannot verbalize. This was Gaia awakening and the Indigo mind tuning into her frequency.

Indigo, the mighty word. When I was asked to write this book, it was evident to me that this was going to be a confession book, where I would highlight my journey and awakening as an Indigo child. I decided that I would not dwell on the word itself or what it meant since it had been so extensively covered. Rather, I would speak of my journey as Alexander, a young man like any other who had experienced the loss of one side of himself, giving way to the rebirth of another, with the Indigo child energy as a backdrop. I believe that the message lies in the journey and in the most elusive moments that characterize it. I wanted to convey what it meant to be an Indigo child, from the beginning to the now, from the perspective of my life and its lessons. The collective journey would be the one to bring the truth to the surface. Through my ups and downs, my downfall and new beginnings, other Indigos could find their own experiences, their truths juxtaposed to the ones I highlight here. It was important to speak of a personal human journey in the modern world, that lead to hope and love against all odds so that others could understand from their own voyages. We are all one, whether we like to admit it or not, all human beings, all from the Source. Only when we lay things bare, the truth unequivocal, and we open ourselves up to others can we relate to each other, and our experiences do not go to waste within the continuum of life. I promised myself this, a simple account of an extraordinary journey, the story of human life the way it really is and of what could be if the heart were open. It was an understanding with my guides that I would reiterate my journey and the truth I had extracted from it as a human being first, as an Indigo Child second. I would be both regardless. I would relay my journey in its simplest form so as to convey it fluidly. And so I began.

My exploration continued and increasingly meshed with my life in a symbiotic manner, existing on both planes and in both realities. There were episodes that confused and blurred the separation between the two: nightly encounters with foreign energies and voyages farther and more profound than any that came before. I would rise the next day wondering if it was all a dream. I knew that this was only healthy doubt and should not be regarded with too much importance. It all took a turn for the better as I renewed my contact with the Arcturians. I was now more mature and able to understand and process our encounters. There were intervals between our sessions, though they were getting more frequent. With our renewed communication, I went through some initiations whereby. I would enter deep trances and be given vast amounts of information as per the true nature of dimensions and the universe, and how they merged with the concept of time. This would go on for a week and then halt. Within one or two months it had finished and I had established a much closer bond with Jimmael as a space brother that watched over me at all times. I was asked to meet him on the physical plane on a certain night.

At the time I lived in a suburb of Tel-Aviv, with a cul-de-sac behind my building. Adjacent was a wild hill. It was totally isolated and felt like an isle of peace that looked over the entire city. I was told we would meet there at night. In truth, it could be eerie considering the circumstances. There was fog in the skies, an aftermath of rain, and the cold coupled with humidity seeped into your bones. I went there as I was asked. I cannot deny that I was somewhat petrified due to the setting and the prospect of finally meeting a being from another time and place. I must have waited there for two hours, trying to get to terms with my faith and what was happening. Shivers ran up my spine until I decided to leave. Nothing had happened. I was upset and demanded an explanation but I knew better than channel when angry and tired, as it would affect the purity of the message I was to receive. The next day I called Shlomit. She explained to me that I had indeed experienced something with Jimmael, that he was there but not in a capacity that I could see, especially when shrouded with doubt, fear, and ego. I later found out that our space brothers sometimes manifested themselves in ways that were not visible to the eye but nonetheless were there. The shivers I had felt, beneath the cold, damp expression of fear, was the energy I sensed so close by. I was told I still had to work on my ego and balancing my willpower for this to happen in a correct way. All later encounters, as they intensified, would be totally unexpected so as not to allow me to demand anything. With time, I would learn and establish a new- found trust in the awakening process, whereby, as everything had already happened in the continuum of time, I only had to believe that it would occur when it was right. It did.

Much information had been shared with me but I admit it was more important for me to personally get to know them better and establish a basis of faith in this chapter of my life. Jimmael was ever present in my awakening, part of the guidance that appeared in my channelings congratulating me on my progress and sharing his love for me. He was from far away, a place that existed only in my imagination, a future version of Terra. He was alien to me in his physicality and the version of reality he existed in but he was so close to me beyond these notions. He was and is a brother, always there, always guiding, always reinforcing the positive in everything. I must highlight that beyond the formality of his messages and the very clear way that they are conveyed, I have never heard him iterate notions of a glass half empty. Everything is a process, all is meant for growth. There are no wrongs or mistakes, because we emerge from them with a new understanding and appreciation for the circumstances that created them in the first place. The mistakes we make are thus a blessing in disguise. I am more and more appreciative for all the pain I felt, for all my shortcomings, my failures, and my addictions. I am in a privileged position of awareness and understanding and I could not have done any of this without my "wrongdoings." Perhaps wrong is the new right or perhaps they are the same, just different sides of the same coin.

As I moved on with my life, our encounters became more powerful and vivid. I would later move to a new apartment, bringing forth new experiences with the Arcturians. They would now physically manifest themselves as lights in the sky. I would sit in the attic with my window open to the dark night sky, only to witness bright green lights that would appear out of nowhere, reflect upon buildings, and disappear. I would try to rationalize where they came from or from whom, but to no avail. They would blaze a trail up above me as I made my way home at night from work, appearing and disappearing seconds later, in white, yellow, or green hues. They were as vivid as the red flash that I had witnessed months ago at the hands of Yahweh. They were to become more and more frequent, always accompanied by a message or as a token of appreciation for a spiritual process I was going through. The most vivid remains a session I had with Shlomit as we worked on balancing my ego.

We were sitting on the roof of my apartment after nightfall, enclosed by walls and covered by a bamboo pergola. There was only us and the skies above. It was crystal clear with the stars each shining their own light upon the canvas of night. We were talking before beginning the meditation. Suddenly, I witnessed a green flash of light appear and disappear just as quickly a few meters from the edge of the roof. My skepticism asked me to rationalize and I looked for a teenager flashing a green laser at the sky, but I knew better. Light photons would have to be reflected off a surface so as to be seen, otherwise light would simply keep on moving forward at a speed we cannot grasp. The sky offered no such base for it to reflect. Soon another appeared above us within the confine of the roof. It was closed from all sides so I knew that it was for real as no light could enter such high walls. Shlomit feared for an instant as she had never witnessed this. She told me she was glad we were experiencing this together, and so did I. She felt safe this way and I felt assured that it was really happening.

The lights shone one final time right above us and vanished. It was a sign. She began to channel. She said it was from an extraterrestrial race that I knew. She did not know their name. "Arcturus," I said. "Yes!", her eyes lit up. They had come to learn about the ego and what it meant. It was the first time I had heard them speak through another person, or in Hebrew for that matter. They had learned the language since our contact began although I still feel more comfortable speaking to them in English. It was the final reinforcement that I needed in order to understand, through manifestation on the physical plane, that all the "conversations" I was having in my head for the last two years were real. This was very symbolic for me. I had faith no matter what the circumstances were, but it would often feel like insanity to have these contacts with different intelligences and beings within the confines of my inner voice. Many times did I ask myself if it was all a dream. Would I be more comfortable just existing on the physical plane? Perhaps. Beyond that moment, there was no more room for that. It was gone. I was either to believe or to live in a limbo of doubt forever more.

With this affirmation, I slowly had a newfound appreciation for the small things in life. I had for so long, wanted the world to change instantly and expected the New Age to bring about new beginnings almost overnight. I expected to no avail. By now, I had learned to take the moment as it came, secure in the fact that things were changing at their own peace, just as I had developed at mine. This gave me a reason to appreciate my existence, even the dire circumstances. I understood that life was a game. I do not wish to underplay the serious tones that it can take. What I mean is that within this physical experience, once you are privy to witness its spiritual counterpart and understand what it means to live, you can appreciate even the smallest, most trivial things. It is all part of the human experience. Everything we encounter on this journey, and I mean this in a physical sense, is an experience. We are here to experiment with the limits of our perspective of said reality. This means everything is simply a manifestation of reality, just like in the online virtual world, where you are studying before a screen pretending to be someone within a game. I knew who I was, where I came from, where life would eventually take me, and what the world was ultimately facing. I knew I would get to know even more, so why not take more pleasure in the simple little things of daily life that seemed mundane otherwise? Take your dog for a long enjoyable walk, learn how to cook, take interest in how technical things work, read, educate yourself, or even fall in love. On that journey, as long as we respect other people, there is no wrong or right. We can eat, drink, taste and experience anything and every-thing even for an instant. Dive into seas of people, polar op-posites of you, sample other cultures, meet significant others of any creed or race, and take an interest in anything quirky and offbeat. Make love as if it were the last time and sample every food as if you could never again eat anything. It is an experience, a glorified game with unfortunate consequences if we push too far. There are confines of daily life, yes. There are rules, regulations, and time frames. Yet beneath, above, and between these, there is space to live, and not conduct ourselves as if the world of today is a copy of the one yesterday and the one of tomorrow. Every day is a question mark and demands experience even on the smallest level. This is part of living, the reason why people with endless curiosity live a full and rewarding life, and those who take everything for granted and see only repetition become victims of their points of view. While you experience your highest moments be thankful for all the Creator has given you. Remember these instants and all the positives leading to them when you are experiencing a low. Life is a cycle. The wheel always turns, valleys become mountains, and then valleys once again. All we can do is change the intervals. I have had the pleasure of meeting very physical people along the way with not a trace of spirituality, that embraced life and learned from it in such a way that they could have been the most aware people you could encounter. They lived in the moment and knew the nature of love and appreciating what it gives us. They understood a lot of things I realized I still had to learn, just like that. Find these people and befriend them. You will thank yourself later.

It was well into 2011 by now. I had more of a sense of self, of awakening, and of what it meant to be me. The intervals between slumps of faith were increasingly farther apart and although I understood I still had a lot to learn, I was enriched by all that I had experienced until now. I had felt much older than my age as I went through my early awakening process, sometimes feeling like a human Atlas in bearing the burden of my pain and all the knowledge I had received. I could now release all that negativity and embrace the moment through the child that lived within me. I felt as if I had experienced a swoon of youth permeating my reality. All was fresh and new ripe for the picking. It was often hard to believe I was only 27 years old, for I had witnessed myself through the ages since my inception as a being that transcended time.

This brings me to an important point about Indigos. They are old souls, older than you can fathom. They have their own version of reality and how the world should be and they stick to it. Essentially, however young and belligerent they may be and no matter the envelope they arrive in, they are wiser than their years and the things they claim to know come from a place far across the ages. They have returned to put into effect the knowledge they possess and clear the karmas of Atlantis and Lemuria we have as a collective consciousness. This knowledge, regardless of how you regard or disregard it as a youthful indiscretion to be addressed with Ritalin and other mind-numbing medication, will bring forth a day when the veil lifted. Then, you will understand what they were meant for. We have a hierarchy in society, a very clear one at that. Sadly, enough, it is not a meritocracy, based on human achievement, but a rule of mental arrogance. We require all beings to have studied extensively and to rise to a certain socio-economic level for us to listen to them. We accept only those who have studied and acquired amounts of linear knowledge, as we deem this to be the solution for our worldly problems. We elect our governmental representatives according to their careers, not their humanity or integrity. The same goes for the management of large companies. We would never consider entering into a discussion about important things, adult matters, with a teenager. All teenagers are regarded as still in their infancy in terms of life experience and ability to deal with it. They are not taken seriously as beacons of knowledge. Only when they become the bright minds of the future, perhaps developing radically new technological solutions, do we listen. What if we were to accept that the knowledge that the ruling adults of today have is basically the reason the planet is in such a dire situation socially, economically, and environmentally? What if we accepted that the notions of yore are now outdated, like a typewriter juxtaposed to a brand new laptop, and that the world has witnessed an upgrade in human evolution through these youths and those to come? They are not equipped to deal with the strict mores and values of today. This is absolutely true, and why we see an increase in attention deficit disorders and learning "disabilities ". It is not a curse but a blessing. Their entire physical constitution is geared for something else entirely. They can understand the most complex abstract ideas like deciphering computer code, but have a difficult time rationalizing redundant modern-day ideals. The truth is that knowledge, at the soul level, transcends all else, especially numeric age. If we do not change our outlook on life and where humanity is going, there will be none within the next fifty years. Were we to open ourselves and our conscious minds to younger thoughts and hear what they have to say about the status quo, we might find solutions that an archaic mindset could never iterate. Nonetheless, it is happening, when we use Google, Instagram, while surfing the matrix of the Web, or as we witness a new generation of bright businessmen and women that are the age you were when you entered college. They are bright, think at warp speed, and can tackle anything you throw at them as long as it is properly motivating and challenging. The Indigo generation is firmly anchored in our reality. Its pioneers came long before you knew they existed, as far back as 100 years ago, to lay the groundwork. The main waves came in the late 1980s to early the 2000s, but there were individuals before that. Not everyone born before, during, or after will be from this frequency. Many of my generation are Indigos, some older than me, and many younger. The crescendo occurred later and halted as we entered the 21 century. Some are textbook cases, while others are much more complex, as well as older, making it harder to identify. The idea is not to dwell on the details, but to acknowledge this movement as it changes our reality, and to accept that older generations are not omnipotent and all-knowing. If they were the world would paint a much brighter picture. Listen to the youths of today and accept them as equals. Do not turn your back on them because your birth date occurred mid-20th century. You would be passing on an abundance of knowledge that you could benefit from. Someone once told me that a wise man knows that he knows nothing at all. This is definitely the case. Accept that this new reality is not something you can grasp unless you are willing to listen and learn, even from our youth. The future is now.

A second wave of encounters occurred simultaneously with my experiences with Jimmael. Yahweh of the Elohim had returned and bestowed a task on me. I was to work with the collective consciousness of humanity in reuniting it with its feminine side, the more compassionate and loving energy which it so yearned for. I would complete this in a long meditation, clearing its karma from overpowering masculine ideals. Yahweh announced to me that upon the completion of my journey of healing with Gaia, and humanity, I would be asked to continue helping other civilizations that existed parallel to ours, also in a state of spiritual development in other universes and galaxies. I accepted and said I was ready. Yahweh asked me if I could start now and I answered with a definitive yes. Do not bite more than you can chew. Over the next few nights, I would leave my body while asleep and follow tremendous voyages into galaxies I had never known of. I cannot recount all that happened during this time, only the broad scope of it. We would eventually communicate while I was conscious and went on a journey together. He told me we would go to the Central Sun of the Universe where he was based, to meet the other Elohim. It was extremely vivid and powerful. We travelled through endless vortexes in time and space, popping up in one place only to enter another portal and emerge somewhere else entirely. Eventually, we ended up in the Central Sun, the place where the Source energy exists in its fullest form. We entered an etheric chamber much resembling a board room. The Elohim surrounded it, all resembling wise, old men, tall in stature and beaming with white light. It was the first time I had such a clear and structured encounter. I literally felt as if I was there. It reached much further than visualization through my third eye. They told me that, if I was willing, I could begin helping them with future endeavors concerning other civilizations that were awakening as well. I accepted. I was told that it was part of who I was, as I had guided them when they were like us, long before linear time existed. They were happy to be cooperating again. Most of the work would be done while I slept so as not to disturb my cycles. I was happy to be on my merry way to new experiences beyond my perception. What and whom would I encounter? Over the next week, I barely managed to sleep, witnessing all sorts of mishaps in my physical reality. I believed it was part of the burden, a side effect of sorts. This situation only worsened. Eventually, I called Shlomit, who alarmed me by telling that all this work had resulted in part of my soul being dispersed all over the place, meaning that even as I awoke, when the soul is meant to return to the body, only a fraction was actually. This is when I realized my eagerness had caused this and that I had bitten off more than I could chew. She guided me through the phone, asking all the parts of my being to return to the here and the now and cutting off all ties to the Elohim, for the time being. I thanked Yahweh for the opportunity and vowed I would help him when I was ready but not before. He was very compassionate and understanding. It was difficult for me but I was relieved. It was as if I had failed, not living up to the expectations I had for myself. Today, I understand there is a time and place for everything in this world and it is never where and when it suits us, but when you are truly ready. It was a very valuable lesson, not to let my ego engage me in things that were beyond my grasp as I was barely ripe. I thanked the Creator for its protection and resumed my daily life, free of this tumultuous voyage into the unknown.

After this chapter of exploring the metaphysical world by myself, I had rekindled my connection with Shlomit who remains until today a "soul sister." She has helped me through hard times when I needed guidance the most, and has been able to address the essence of my most difficult moment with little effort. We have helped each other through sessions when we could use our mutual energetic resources to solve one another's problems. I believe that regardless of how gifted anyone may be, he or she will always need teachers and guides in whatever form they may come forward. We often need only to be pointed in the right direction to unravel our otherworldly gifts. I had spent a long chapter of my awakening without any contact with members of the group I was once part of, scouring the infinite consciousness by myself. The time came when I had to deal with deeper issues, behavioral patterns that had to change and needed guidance from a different perspective to address them correctly. This was around the same time when we renewed contact. It was always amazing to me how another human being could be so selfless and thrive from the energy of giving, without ever asking for anything in return. This was Shlomit. Unparalleled love and selflessness we could all benefit from. She would always rise to the occasion when I had hit an impasse and needed a boost over that hurdle. She is also very much an Indigo Child, and the person who is the most connected to herself that I have encountered so far, always able to listen to the voice from within without interruption. I have learned much from her, but I would like to recount on two occasions that I consider life-changing. These sessions enabled me to let go of the most destructive patterns that existed in my life.

I have discussed anger before, that emotion that is all-encompassing and ravages all the senses like a volcanic eruption, uncontrollable and destructive from within outwards. I had always been overwhelmed by my anger, never really learning how to control it and what it meant to me. As I had reflected in my darkest hour, I knew it was not solely anger or rage. It was not hatred for my predicament but something much deeper and more elusive. It would come out of me in a wave that, when peaked, would be almost impossible to come down from. I knew this since I was very young, explosive at the sight of injustice or lies. As I got older it took another dimension and became violent and destructive, to myself and those around me. I would always shudder at the thought of confrontation of any kind as I was afraid what my reaction would be. It was always unpredictable. It would build up in a way not appeasable and erupt, many times ending in violence. This could happen anywhere. As you get older you begin to understand the consequences of your actions. These worsen when you reach adulthood and are able to calculate the outcome before you begin, much like a game of chess. Therefore, there is always an inner last resort alarm that tells you that you have entered dangerous territory beyond a certain point. The unfortunate thing is to allow it to get to that point. Reasoning is much more of a feasible solution and you are able to exit any such encounter unscathed. As I had reached a stage in my life when I didn't care about it anymore, all these consequences lost their value. Situations had become direr and emotions disproportionate. The thing that worried me the most was how it was eating at me. Many dark nights did I spend stewing in my anger, almost feeling as if it consumed me like a flame from within. I honestly did not think that I would make it to my 30th birthday this way. I assumed that I would eventually succumb to this emotional lava. I lived with it for so long that it had become a part of me. It had carried on through my Awakening albeit to a much lesser degree, and with entirely new intervals between episodes. The anger was fading slowly but there were still traces of it. It was geared towards humanity, people that had vanished when my situation took a turn for the worse and my family, with whom I had no contact for almost 3 years. With time, I had transcended this reality into a new one, made peace with these elements in my life and was slowly learning what forgiveness really meant. I am still in awe of individuals who beat the odds and are capable of forgiving people who have caused them the greatest, most unspeakable harm, whether physical or emotional, and who are able to wholesomely embrace these people with unequivocal love. The fact that they can surpass all their emotions and reach a state where they thank their "aggressors" for what they have taught them, with sincere appreciation is remarkable. I believe they are saints in their own right, able to rise above all their traumas and embrace a state of perpetual love. As I began to understand what love and forgiveness meant, there were still traces of that anger along the way, and I recognized that it was something more than what it seemed. I knew well that I would have to relinquish any expectations from people as this would lead nowhere. Each person is a universe in themselves with their own preconceptions and ideals, no matter how different from yours and mine. They behave accordingly and this does not change often, no matter how much you would like them to see things your way. They are not you, and even though you may be convinced that your point of view is the penultimate truth, they have built their own through circumstances, fears, and mores they were exposed to. Along with this comes their karmic baggage only to set them more apart from you. It took me an eternity to understand this notion of personal truth which I will cover later.

Back when I was studying in the center, my guides reiterated something over and over. I had taken the karmic debts of my parents in this lifetime. My suffering and the distance it put between us was meant to clear their karmas and make them understand its roots. A told me I was what Judaism calls a Tsadik, which was difficult to accept being that I tried to distance myself from religion as a whole. It meant, for lack of a better word, "righteous one," one who takes upon themselves the karmic load of the consciousness of others in order to awaken them. I understood it and it made sense to me but I asked myself repeatedly why I would have done such a thing, especially if it didn't change much. On one hand, this explained much to me. It gave me a greater understanding of my pain, the reason it began within the nucleus of the family and why I had to endure the long, hard road to awakening alone. That being said, it made me expect in many ways that they would awaken to the new reality the world presented them and that it would alter the status quo. This did not happen for the most part. They were forced to accept me for who I am, and to respect the journey I had made to get to this point through my self-sustenance. I was wrong to expect anything to change. I had only taken the burden upon myself once again instead of accepting others as they are, for better or worse. Eventually, we were reunited and eating at the same table again. Things were better overall, but my anger still lurked in the shadows.

Shlomit was over at my house on a summer evening in 2011. We were going through a session to close chapters and karmas that remained active. We went through a list of my addictions and made little notes with Reiki symbols on them, thanking the Creator for them being healed. I was to undertake this for a month, daily, channeling healing to these notes until they disappeared on their own or I felt better. Eventually, though I do not recall exactly how, we got to the issue of my anger. I expressed my concern about how it was not what I thought, and I wanted to know its root at the most ancient and primal core. Once and for all, I wanted to recall and feel what lead to this unfortunate behavioral pattern that had marked me for so long. I went into a trance and asked to see the first time it originated. It took me to a time much before time existed. There I was able to balance my karma with the Creators' light and project it forward through time to the present as if it had never existed. As I finished this, I began to channel a message from the Creator. It explained to me the origin of this emotion and why it was so acute. The answer I was given was ludicrous but it made sense on some level. It explained that I was created at a time when only endless light existed. There were few beings at that time, only seas of the same energy towards infinity. Beings of light were given a purpose and a task in the greater scheme of things. My anger came from my perceived fallibility of the Creator. It was long before there was such a thing as ego, but it certainly sounded like a precursor. The main idea was that we were made as the children of the Creator and had, much like we do with parents, an impression of its omnipotence and infallibility. As we matured and expanded our own consciousness through the exploration of free will, I began to get a sense of its all-encompassing energy and the implausible finite nature of its infinity. As I pondered on this endless white light, it seemed as if it was finite since it was basically a repetition of itself endlessly. This sparked certain anger at the "illusion" it had created as per its godliness. This means, though it seems ridiculous to me today, that the mere idea that you could measure and entertain the notion of its being contradicted the seemingly infinite energy, as if I had sized it up and become disappointed with the fact that I was able to do so in the first place. Please imagine this in very abstract terms of infinity. There were only waves of energy parallel to each other floating in an endless continuum, a wave in itself, with no beginning or end. I tried to anthropomorphize this vision in order to understand it, but it made it even more incredulous so I left it in its purest form. Basically, it was some kind of etheric rebellion. It is indisputable that the Creator's energy is endless as is its love, but it took me the fall from grace and the endless lifetimes that lead to the present to understand this. Since there was "nothing" but light then it was easy to question the nature of it all and what lay beyond. I did not know better as there was nothing else to know. This transcended through the ages as a sort of existential rage. Today, it was directed at the world, at the way I expected it to be as opposed to the way it was, at my predicament, my pain, my disappointment in human nature, and the current state of the planet. I believe a lot was directed towards me as well. I had wanted more than it had to give and had to finally close the cycle only at this time, within this very physical body of a 27-year-old human man. I was angry at myself for the long, hard road taken, and for making everything so difficult, but how else could I understand what was really important without losing everything, shedding a skin, and growing a new one made of light? That day I released all that anger and its extensions, and accepted where it came from and what it had taught me, I thanked it and it was gone. For the first time in my life I was in control of this. This was the closure of the first important chapter of my old life, under Shlomit's watchful eye.

It was now the fall of 2011. I was entertaining the need for a vacation and wanted to return to Greece after an exodus of almost three years. It was a return to the source where it all began, as well as rekindling old relationships and releasing those that had run their course. It was a huge step over a short distance, much more than a mere holiday. I had visited Greece the Easter prior for 4 days that reiterated the pain I had gone through 4 years before, and I was out of balance my entire stay there. I needed this to be different. I knew there was something that had to change in my perception of things. I needed to close the 4-year cycle I had gone through since I had left so that I could begin anew. I asked Shlomit over for a last session to free me from my past predicament. She came over promptly, uttering the word I did not want to hear: "**EGO**." This was coincidentally the encounter we shared with the Arcturians, who had come to learn about this word. We all have one, some are more pronounced than others. They, unfortunately, manage to run most of us. I had done work in all areas of my life, scouring my endless consciousness but had evaded this for very long. This deserves a book of its own, or maybe an encyclopedia. I will get into its nature later but it deserves a proper introduction. The ego is today an innate part of us. It is best to think about it in terms of its own consciousness with its own agenda. It is and always will be within us. The best we can do is make peace with it and put it in its place. It is the little voice that always whispers within our ears the things we want to hear, but not the ones we need to hear. We are never wrong. We are all-knowing, victimized, pushed into the margins, and never accountable for any of our actions. It is what puts us in defensive mode, what pushes us through life with a survivalist outlook, and what makes us weak and weary when we want others' pity. It is set on making sure that it preserves itself along with us as a host through the most difficult times, and it is not very adept at letting go of old mindsets. It was something I knew I would have to go through one day but had neglected. I can safely say it was the most important lesson to date, and it would change my life by giving me the reins back. Many times I had been overburdened by that voice inside which wanted me to embrace fear, to repeat patterns which I was tired of, to believe everything was about survival, and that my stubbornness was the right way to solve things, never accepting my wrongdoings. It ran my life for very long and even after studying about it, I never really understood what it meant. I was at an old friend's house about a month ago. We were talking about spirituality, and the topic of ego came up. He proceeded to Pick up a book he was reading. It was called "Eastern Wisdom" by Zen Master Nissim Amon. He read me a chapter about crows. The crow was an analogy for the Ego, always cawing in any given situation. There was the crow that entered the scene as we were trying to fall asleep, another for when we wanted others to pity us or to elevate ourselves above others. They were many, and they were always there. This was a simple enough explanation of what the ego is but accurate, to say the least. It is and always will be there. I went through that session with Shlomit learning to recognize it and returning to the time it was created in a previous life. I cleared what had led to this and proceeded to make peace with it as best I could. I listened carefully to all the scenarios it could appear in and understood that it had been running me for too long. It was there to knock me off my pedestal when I felt elated, making sure I switched to worrying immediately. It was there to make sure I blamed others for my misfortunes. It was the voice that made me think I was going insane in my darkest hour. From that moment I learned to spot it in every-day life and make sure it didn't interfere any longer. Could I control it? That was the question. Every creature has a master and this applies to the Ego as well. I learned to talk to it sensibly when I could, and put it in the corner, in my mind's eye, like a decadent youth as soon as I saw it rearing its ugly pout up and about. This was a great realization as I could stop myself from descending into states of mind that were no longer befitting my spiritual awakening. It was comical to shush it but it worked. The crow no longer cawed, its beak taped shut. It tried but mostly in vain. This was a new dimension of awareness. I was able to sense it as it tried to invade my positivity at any given time, and avoid the consequences. I was aware of the voice inside that did not benefit this process. I will not deny it has sudden comebacks, like an outdated rock band, but is quickly shut down. This took time over the next couple of months 2011 was ending and I made my way to Greece. I was elated, able to feel awakened and renewed in the place where it all began. I was told that this step had closed the 4-year awakening process I had undertaken, and I was ready to begin a new chapter. It was literally like travelling into the past and re-experiencing what it had to give you: the sights, sounds, and encounters, all while in a new state of awareness with knowledge and wisdom I did not have before. I could experience the past and present juxtaposed as I treaded in between them, a reminder of who I was and who I had become in this short time. I could see the transformation even physically, and could let go of my past life, embracing who I was in the world of today. I renewed my connection with old friends, family, and my surroundings, finding a new appreciation for this society as it entered the most trying chapter in its modern history. I could now see what others saw in Greece, the survival, the savoir-faire, the love of life. It is such a spiritual place that understands the undercurrent of life without ever knowing of it. Life happens by the instant and not beyond, and is celebrated as if it were the last. I fell in love with it, its people's resilience and their warmth all anew. It was as though I had never left. I was also elated at the fact that it had transpired exactly as my guidance had told me. I had gone through the entire experience with only the Creator to guide me. I found faith there with all this physical feedback, as my fear of the unknown was eradicated with this successful return to the past. I had left only to return to the most painful place for me, led by faith that it was the right thing to do. It was all of my spiritual guidance manifesting itself in this physical scenario, showing to me one final time that miracles do happen by way of believing. There was no more room for skepticism. It was the final proof that I needed. My "reality beyond reality" existed and had very physical repercussions. I returned to Israel in October, ready to embrace the coming of this new age. I welcomed me with a surprise: a message from my deceased grandfather. He was proud of who I had become, my strength and resolve, and what I was meant to give the world. I was told me he belonged to a group called The Council of Elders, a group of etheric beings that kept universal knowledge, only coming down to the physical plane with a specific task, and seldom so. He told me he had been watching over me since the day I was born into this world and awaiting my rebirth. He ended by telling me he was always here and guiding me from beyond. I felt his presence around as the hairs on the back of my neck stood erect as a ruler. I have kept this message dearly as it combines both worlds for me. It is the spirit of a man who once walked this earth before I came to be, but who is for me as physical as the resonance he left in my surroundings. He is as real as anyone else and I hold his memory dearest to my heart, even more than what he symbolizes for me.

The days passed quickly and ushered in the date of the beginning of the Ascension. This was the time we had all been waiting for, what the Christians referred to as "The Rapture." It came about on the 11ᵗʰ of November 2011, 11-11-11, at 11:11 am and throughout the day. It was a global celebration, entertained in a meditation by many spiritual groups all over the world. They had a higher vibrational frequency than their less spiritual peers and therefore were closer to reaching this, provided they had agreed to ascend. The main groups were the Indigo and Crystal children, the following generation. This would separate those willing to change and ascend in vibration and those still stuck in a 3D state of mind. I will not deny that there are many types of souls upon this planet, some angelic, some extraterrestrial, and many humans. The human souls are the most recent creations of the Creator, specifically to populate the planet when it was needed, and are somewhat younger and less experienced. Therefore, this would make Ascension potentially more difficult for them. That being said, as the Creator gave all of us the equal right to choose, the possibilities are endless. The Metatron had once been a human being with no relation to the spiritual hierarchy, as are all the Ascended Masters at the beginning, so there is always a possibility. The Age of Ascension had drawn many of the highest beings ever created to incarnate, many as Indigo children in order to usher in this New Age and implement the necessary changes. They would destroy the sickly foundations of the world and rebuild them, leaving it to the Crystal Children to re-educate humanity as per the principles of the Creators' love. As the planet is linked to the human consciousness, only after the final choice was made by the rest whether to ascend or not would the anchoring in the 5ᵗʰ density be final. For now, the ascended ones were reborn on this new plane while the rest still existed in the space between dimensions, an infinity in itself. After the anchoring was over, those refusing to ascend would be existing with 3rd-dimensional awareness in a 5th-dimensional world, whereby all their fears and worries would become real in an instant. All it takes to make the switch is not to fight the tides, but to realize nothing is eternal except the soul, and to release all that is no longer right for you. You must understand that changes are necessary. If certain areas of your life are blocked to no avail, they require to letting of old mindsets and embracing new ones in order for a new path to reveal itself. Trust that embracing the unknown of 5D will only bring forth abundance. As the clock hit 11:11 am I entered into a deep trance. I elevated my entire being into the 5th dimension and cut all ties to those beneath me. I recreated myself there and agreed to release all fears and worries pertaining to the past, all obsolete mindsets, and affirm this beginning sequence in my new life. I thanked the Creator for all that it had given me and embraced the Universe, grateful ahead of time for all the abundance that it would put in my path. After I had virtually recreated myself, I proceeded to bring that wave of energy down onto the physical plane and release it like a wave with me at the center, changing my reality in an instant. Half an hour later it was over and I resumed my daily activities, permeated in new awareness. "The New Age is here," I reflected upon with a broad smile. I knew all well that my physical reality would not change since it had not elevated itself along with me, and that the changes in abilities and awareness would take their time. This was a gradual awakening of the entire physical and etheric structure, but I was embracing this New Age as I stood before a sea of endless possibilities. Another two months passed and 2011 became 2012, the year the world would end. At least it would end as we know it. I ushered in the New Year and the New Age in a deep meditation. I was channeling the Creator at the same time. It told me that it was an age of infinity. I had not to worry about anything anymore since the impossible was now possible. All I had ever imagined was now at arms' length. I would live to see great change, a metamorphosis of humanity and its foundations, as we entered an era of new creation. I was in a stark white room, dressed in white, where the outline of everything meshed with infinity. I took a seat in a white chair. Before me, there was a screen or a window looking out at the infinity of space. It was what was to come. I had tears in my eyes as I realized the changes to occur. The truth would finally be revealed. The message echoed in my mind not to worry, to have faith in the work I had done and the changes I had brought about as I peered into this vastness. That sight would become my screensaver for life. It was so real. I was looking at my Higher Self, an image as crisp as looking in the mirror. I was sensing the universe open up as I let this vision permeate my physical reality in 2012. I realized the version of me in the chair was how I really was beyond the confines of the body, the home, and the immediate reality. It was me, endless as the universe, as we all are, understanding that every second is an opportunity for renewal and change. The other me greeted me with a smile and a welcome. I was there…now. The future is here now, dreaming is now living.

5.

Truisms for a New Time

I HAVE LEARNED AN enormous amount of things these past years. I am not the same person anymore. I have changed, as has the world around me. If I could pass one last thing on it would be the specific notions I accepted that changed me as a human being. They are axioms we all know, mundane ideas that took on new meaning as I explored the hidden sides that we do not encounter during our lives. I would like to trace them back, one by one, to gain a deeper understanding of what the things we perceive as obvious really mean to tell us about ourselves and our reality.

TRUTH

A truth is somewhat of an axiom, a universal idea that is in itself self-evident and becomes a standard for what is real and what is not. It is a measure we use to distinguish the two when we deem something to be true, or not to be. Can we measure ourselves by this standard? Is there a universal bank of truths that pertains equally to us, as some things in mainstream thought are real and others not? What about personal truth? What is it? How does it relate to a universal truth? Is it true that the sky is blue and not true that it is purple? It is true that there is a difference in the physical composition of a male and that of a female. Is it true because it is? It is anchored in our physical reality and it is visible, therefore acceptable as true. This is what the world embraces the most. I see therefore I believe. How does this apply to your personal version of the truth? Perhaps there are universal axioms and then more personal versions of those. It begets the question of what it means to be you. Who am I? I believe it to be a self-evident truth that I am who I am. Or is it more complicated?

I can say that my quest started with truth, not finding out the truth but avidly pursuing my own. First I had to discover it. I was amidst a cloud of self-doubt while beginning my journey, abiding by what I then believed to be my truth. This set me so far apart from those around me until they were no longer in my life, since I could not accept their hypocrisy and the duality of their truth. I set about to find myself and establish the totality of my own truth, only to understand much later what it really meant. I never felt accepted by those around me, especially family, since I was different. Many times did my truth clash with their beliefs, casting me in self-doubt, and many times did I try to mask it only to feel like I betrayed myself. The bottom line is the affirmation of self: I am who I am. It is the most important lesson in life, since to be accepted you must accept yourself. To do this, in turn, you must ask: "Who am I?" It is the penultimate existential question that seems more nebulous than anything else, but there is a definite answer. Unfortunately, only one person can provide that answer: YOU. We live in a world of ultimate truths and dogmas. Some are "right" and the rest are "wrong," and those abiding by the latter are morally on the wrong side of the tracks. I will definitely endorse the fact that some things are true in that they ensure the sanctity of everyone's truth, like the fact that no one should kill or sacrifice another human being.

I was exposed to a new version of truth while in college, in a sociology course. It called for **Cultural Relativism** as an ideal that embraces and respects the other as having their own truth. It basically argues that every culture on the globe has their own dogma, mores, and truths, and that they are as important as the mainstream points of view we have in the West. In no way is the way we see things in our modern Westernized world better or more applicable than what another culture embraces. They believe in what they believe, and that belief system makes them who they are. Everything is relative one to another just like black is to white. We can argue that white is the color of light and therefore it is better than black or that black is the color of darkness, with no relation to any racial epithets. The truth is that they exist only in contrast to one another. They cannot ideologically exist without the other one to use as a comparative basis. The notions that we attribute to these are what we create and imagine for each one. Therefore, they do not really exist. They are mere ideals. This does not stop us from arguing that white is better than black and perpetrating this notion forth. The same goes with Western ideals of democracy versus other nations. They may seem more primitive to a Westerner and therefore less in value, in need of embracing his ideals promptly. The truth is that he does not really know or acknowledge them, nor the principles they stand for. The truth is really grey, so there is no black or white. There is no right or wrong, everything is in proportion to something else. All cultures that are not Westernized have their own notions of truth and reality. There is no argument to be made that one is better than another. We know all too well that great democratic Westernized nations have swarms of problems in their own right. To an Asian person, what they deem to be their culture is their truth, and they may view yours as strange and faulty. So which one is right? Is it the one with the better schooling system and the larger budget where people are seemingly freer? Are they free? There is no answer to that. They are all right and all wrong. The relativism in question means all that we think we know pertains only to us. This notion was revolutionary to me as the media seemed satiated with right and wrong, so adamant on what the world should be even as we witnessed the decline of the West. Democracy was a word used to get things done in a certain fashion to please certain people, but one that in essence was becoming more and more questionable. I do not want to get political as I believe it is only a word that perpetuates illusion through a certain nomenclature. Adhering to strict and familiar notions was only an affirmation of fear, of something that might rattle the foundations of social truth. This is a broad introduction to personal truth. We all are universes in our own right. We are the center of those universes, with all the people in our lives as extensions of us. Imagine this as a sphere with you in the middle. Everything pertaining to you is in this sphere and the way you view things within it is true only to you. Each sphere is as distinct from another as a human iris. We cannot possibly be another person or see the world through their eyes. These spheres connect us through people we know or encounter, in a sort of six of degrees of separation. They all touch somehow but remain separate. In our spheres we exist only to ourselves, to our bodies and to our spirituality. It is said that even the eyesight of every person is not exactly the same in the way we view colors. This is it. We all have our lenses that guide us through life within our spheres, and even as we connect, procreate, and move on, these remain intact. That being said, how can we now tell another person how to live? We simply cannot in any way, shape or form. That person is not us, so we can only share with them the narrow knowledge we have acquired in our own personal sphere. It may or may not help them. If they put too much emphasis on our idea, then they step away from their vision and lose track of how they see the world.

This is how I came to understand truth. Everyone has their own personal truth, that is right only for them. They may or may not be able to share it with others, and maybe they are not supposed to. The point in question is to understand and affirm the existence of this truth. We live in a world of niches, and of group consciousness. We mold our thoughts, decisions, and the pressures of daily life according to these niches. If we do not seem to fit anywhere, we get frustrated and off our path, at least the path we thought we needed to take.

This may prompt us to engage in other's truths to resolve our problems, and further distance ourselves from what is true to us until there is no return. We grow up listening to our parents, our elders and their version of reality even though times change, as do attitudes. We try to swim with the tide as best we can even though we are in the wrong ocean. My identity is integral to my truth, but what is it? It took me very long before I was able to answer this. Only as I was separated from everything that was familiar could I, in the vacuum of my thoughts, answer this question. Who is Alex? What does he look like, wear, like to listen to, believe in, love, and want to do/be? Had I continued to listen to those around me, trying to change for them and morph into another version of myself, I would never have awakened. Awakening meant saying: "This is who I am, what I do, what I believe in, take it or leave it. It is the same to me. I can only be me, nothing else. Alex is so and so and that is all he will ever be. Stomach it, and if you accept it then so be it. If you do not, your loss. I am perfect the way I am. I adhere only to my standards, not yours or society's. I deem myself perfect in all that I am. That is good enough for me. It is who I am. " I realized that as time flew by and I was reunited with those from my past, I was who I was and accepted for it, even revered for standing by my opinions no matter how outlandish or quirky they may be. My faith grew every day to the point that I was able to vocalize opinions that I would have shuddered to even utter in the past. My foundations grew stronger and so did my stance regarding my truth. This is the idea of truth embedded in I AM. IAM WHO I AM. NO APOLOGIES. You are always right in what you choose, whether it is an adequate choice or one that will make you understand something along the way. **Never** let anyone in any capacity tell you that you cannot or shouldn't. It is their fear and preconceptions talking. Our parents' generation has its own vision of the world, what is right and wrong, what is acceptable and correct. Had we always listened to this the world would never have advanced or changed. There would never have been a Feminist movement, a Civil Rights movement, or any other wave that shattered the status quo. As adults, we make one huge mistake. We stop to **dream**. As children, all we do is dream and imagine the unimaginable. As we grow up and are permeated with the truth of our elders, we forget about this. Some do not. We call them musicians, writers, singers, stars of the silver screen, and so on. They venture into the unknown, many times against all odds, only to remind us that we shall dare dream. They create a reality however skewed it may be, as they see it. With time we understand the pioneering at work and brand them geniuses and trailblazers. Everyone can dream and everyone can create. It doesn't have to be a Picasso or a symphony, but we all dream, and who are we without this but mere shadows of our true selves. What is living if we do not pursue those dreams, for they are who we are meant to be? This is part of the Indigo agenda, to shatter notions of self by empowering the youth of this planet. Look at Google or even Wikileaks. They teach us that in this New Age everything is possible. They shatter ideas to make place for new ones, perpetrated by people often too young to drink in the United States. Truth is about empowering the self with an affirmation of who we are unequivocally, of what we want and what we are set on doing. It is the most precious thing to us and defines who we are. You are all you wish to be only if you search for your truth. Be truthful with yourself, do not pretend to be anything else, more or less. You are infinitely perfect to yourself. This is who you are. Make no amends to anyone for it is largely enough. Dream the dream that makes your truth a reality. We are now moving towards 5D, where creating is only a step away. You are the love of the Creator personified, its infinity running through your physicality whether you believe it or not, so how can anyone tell you it is not good enough? Only the person who is himself what he sees in others. You are, have been, and always will be perfection, no matter what you look like, where you are from, what you know or think you do not know. It is your universe. In it, you are the commander of the seas so watch where they take you. Lose the judgmental attitudes and the criticism. Forget the notions of beauty you see in the media, what people are like when they are perfect, and what reflection it has on you. It is only someone else's opinion and their truth, not yours. Eventually, society will change and that person will stay behind, entrenched in their archaic beliefs. Once you can positively affirm you know and accept who you are by loving all of yourself, watch the world around you change by mirroring your love for the new YOU. All the time I spent embracing a truth that was not mine, I would end up feeling physically ill with myself, as if I betrayed who I was. We all have multiple personas for the diverse scenarios that come our way. It is our way of life, and that is fine. At the end of the day, we all have a deeper understanding of who we are whether we address it or not. We can get lost within the charade of personas as much as we want, but we will only get to know ourselves through true, unparalleled appreciation for who we are. I spent a long time negating who I was, to the point that I felt my anger at myself permeate my entire being, until I choked and had to face the music. It doesn't have to be that dramatic. Life is in a constant state of flux, ever-changing. When all the signs point to us letting go of a situation, a dynamic, or a relationship, and we do not listen, it will come back to us from a different angle. It is not a punishment, but a lesson. It is just to show us that there is a clear path and it is being paved for us, by us. Listen to your heart as it tells you to walk down that path. Make no compromise on who you are and do not be afraid to let go because you are apprehensive as to what tomorrow will bring. It is a futile attitude in a liberation scenario. Accept that it is the best thing for you as you look at all the signs along the way. Believe in who you are, and that you are equipped to surface from any obstacle unscathed and wiser. The ultimate truth in life is that we want to return to the Source. There is only love there, so the path points to that, no matter how gloomy the obstacles are along the way. It is an existential choice, but in the end, it is the only way you will ever be whole. You are who you are, no more, no less. Life may be a satyr, but at the end of the act the masks are removed. Do you like and respect the person in the mirror staring back at you? Be love, be truth. Know yourself.

FAITH

Faith is a vessel that carries us through the most difficult times we encounter, when we seemingly have nothing left. We live in a world of incredulity, in which we often do not believe in anything and are forced to rely on our own survival instincts to kick in, and thrust us forward through difficult times. This begets the notion of faith in oneself. To have faith in anything we should first affirm and believe that we are capable of achieving any goal we set out to. The journey to the Soul begins from within. We are often confronted with challenging circumstances that, regardless of religious or spiritual beliefs, force us to examine our reality and what we truly are made of. As we pass through these trying times, we emerge stronger and more determined than ever before. It is adequate when we say that what does not kill us makes us stronger. When we are pushed into the corner we either fold evermore, or we push back. Only then can we know what we are really made of, and the true nature of our strength. It obviously does not have to be so overt, but only in the most difficult situations can an individual really measure his or her worth, as they emerge unscathed from something that would have previously made them shudder. This is a very basic and primal idea of faith in oneself, at the level of believing in one's abilities, inherent or acquired. We must first explore this side, whereby faith in ourselves can guide us through the darkest of times, the sheer belief for even a fragment of a second, that there lies a new reality beyond the hurdles. That brindle of hope is you telling yourself to believe. In turn, that part of you is the Creator's light within you, shining in times of adversity, and reminding you, on a subconscious level, what you are really made of and the origins of this faith. You are an extension of the Creator and its light shines through you with the same intensity. Its love and light are the candles that brighten the path regardless of how austere it may be. Through the concept of faith, there is a tomorrow. The sheer idea that somewhere in the future lies a day that promises us that times have changed and relays that message all the way to the present, is enough for most people. That determination, whether guided by a notion of what you may call God or by pure hope for better days, is the Creator's presence. It is you. Believing in yourself and believing in the Source it is the same thing, whether it is done inadvertently or not. You were created with the greatest attributes, physical and spiritual. These are dormant at this time and going through an awakening. The ultimate version of you is infinity personified. Reflect upon this as you peer at the magnificent vessel it has given you, in the mirror. You were created as perfection in physical form and should regard yourself as nothing less. Affirming this is accepting your godliness, restoring faith in who you are. It has always had faith in you, then why not have faith in yourself? It is all the same in the end. As I survived my most somber hours, I was guided to try and go through another day by that tiny speck of light that lead me, telling me that if there was a moment in the future when all was light, the journey would lead somewhere. This was far before any spiritual awakening, but I, the skeptic, was being guided by the Creator's light and the inner voice that made me surmount another day, and another after that. Today, I realize it paid off and it was divine guidance all along. We all have such days in our lives, so why not accept the prospect of the light and affirm our faith in ourselves? When the tide hits and we are alone, it is all that is left. It is the alpha and the omega. You must believe to see, not see to believe, and the journey towards the infinite light starts with a flicker in the dark. It always shines somewhere within you, whether you believe in it or not. Always remember that.

EGO

A word mystified by modern psychology, probed and over-analyzed without really putting it in terms applicable to one's life. You can choose to be the victim or the captain of your destiny. That depends on who is steering the ship. The ego will always try to take control by imprinting its agenda onto your conscious mind. Affirming yourself and recognizing it will enable you to make it a secondary voice that bears no weight on your decisions. It is indeed a crow, always cawing, but you can just as easily chase it off its branch. Living in this new state of awareness begets making this part of you a peace offering and retiring it. It will always be present within your spiritual construct. It has been effective at pushing you forward, manifesting itself in times of adversity, by elevating you in your mind and seeing life as a competition, making you thrive as you outwitted and outlasted your fellow competitors. At the end, you had advanced out of your old predicament and gained new momentum. Would it allow you to keep it if you kept this frame of mind? This would be a good point to reflect upon. The world has been a survival ground since the fall of Atlantis and Lemuria. We went through dark times, when survival was the only Modus Vivendi and adversity was the only way to come out on top and be able to provide, much like in the animal kingdom. Today, as we enter the New Age, we begin to see the repercussions of all this, the toll it has taken on our bodies, our planet, and our financial reality through the immense gaps in wealth and living standards. Were we to keep this going with greed and Randian objectives in sight, soon enough there would be no world. The world is asking for change. For the collective consciousness to change, it must start with the individual. For you and me to be able to get in touch with our inner voice, our inner truth, we must silence the other voice that keeps on cawing the same behavioral patterns over and over. Out with the old and in with the new. It is a new affirmation of self on the personal plane, and the global. Change starts with you whether you accept it or not. There is no telling if it will try to resurface with time, but how will we know if we can make a difference if we do not recognize it exists and is an integral part of who we are? Where is it really? Where we find doubt, fear, unwillingness to change, self-loathing, self-pity, lack of accountability, and other negative behaviors, you can be sure the ego is present. Beyond getting to know yourself and affirming your truth to circumvent the noise of the ego, you must learn to listen to the heart. It is the only true voice one should pay attention to. It is where channeling and all messages from our spiritual guidance pass through. It is the filter that lets us achieve balance. If we are willing to listen to our own hearts for the answers we seek, distinguishing the right energy from within, we find the truth that resonates with us. We are all born with this gift and can tap into this innately. As channeling is simply tuning into to a certain frequency, the same goes for the voice of the heart. Over time, we can understand the difference between this and the ego. Begin with a simple meditation, quietening everything around you so as to be able to distinctly hear your inner voice. Take, for example, a situation where you have two options: the feeling that one is right versus the over-rationalization that points towards the other. You instinctively know which one you should choose. Take time and listen to both voices speak inside yourself, to their patterns and their message. Let the thoughts take different paths so as to understand which is ego and which is the heart. Put an emphasis on being mindful and listening as opposed to hearing. We can hear anything and everything, but listening means we tune in and lend a closer ear, so as to absorb a given frequency by choice. We filter, as with this matter. It takes time but it is imperative in order to regain control of your conscious mind and be able to make clear-cut, productive decisions. You will sometimes take the long road home out of faith that it will pay off, despite the endless cawing of the ego. Accepting your godliness is another affirmation of self. It means being able to listen to the divine from within, rekindling your relationship with yourself, your truth, your faith, and the Creator. All of this can be done once the ego is put away. You are the master of your fate. Do not believe otherwise; a Creator in your own right. You know what is the right path to take at any given moment, and must do so with certainty and faith, guided by the light from within.

Now that we have painted the ego in the light that we like to see it in, let us address the other side of the coin. We have always seen it portrayed as the culprit for negative outcomes in our lives. The first part of this chapter has outlined how to elevate ourselves above the ego by way of the heart, and tuning into the right frequency to understand things with clarity. The second part is more challenging to accept. The ego is an integral part of who and what we are, and we are quick to believe that it has a mind of its own, keen on disrupting our peace of mind. This could not be further from the truth. The hidden side of the ego is that it manifests itself only per our request, on a spiritual level that is, and mostly unbeknownst to us. I have had many vivid discussions with it over the years and it has repeatedly explained to me that it had presented itself in whatever way at that specific time because I had summoned it at Soul Level, by pursuing the same pattern and not being honest with myself. It will be present, not at times when it is the most uncomfortable for us for its own entertainment, but when we have been repeating a destructive behavior over and over, and we have been adamant to dismiss all signs that it was time to stop and change. Like Saturn, the ego is the one that we perpetually blame for our predicament. The truth is that it is solely here, in its truest form, to expose the issues that need pressing attention, following repeated disregard and victimization from our part. In conclusion, we are not victims. The ego is here to highlight this truth and asks us to take **full responsibility** for ourselves. It asks us to understand that if it is here now it is because we are not listening, and more overt tactics are required. Only through full accountability, coupled with the acquiescence to listen to our heart as the only inner voice, can we rise above our past understanding of things, and affirm our infinity. We are then able to reconcile with it and thank it for its service, as we take over, through said accountability and true introspection. Like this, the next time it would make its appearance we would begin by being grateful it had come, and taking an honest look at what we have been avoiding all along. Let us take responsibility for our present and future by creating through the heart, with the understanding that our entire reality is of our making.

LOVE

Love is light, the light of the Creator. It is ultimately the fabric of its energy, not so much an emotion as a state of being: "Existing in love." It transcends everything and reunites us with the Creator within. It exists above all other, whether positive or negative in polarity. It is from whence we came and that to which we will return. It encompasses compassion, understanding, faith, and truth. See it as a frequency, a **wave** that basks in the Creator's light. It is, in essence, who we are and what we are made of. I do not believe it possible to correctly decipher it as it is as infinite in complexity as the Creator itself. We often confuse our human love for passion, obsession, carnal pursuits, adulation, and other such emotions. They are ultimately fleeting and subjective. This love is universal and more platonic since it exists beyond the idea of gender. I have seldom achieved it during meditation, whereby I felt as if I meshed with the Universe, as if everything was me or I the infinite. I loved it as I love myself, understanding the essence of continuity and infinity. Unfortunately, this feeling elapsed as soon as I had felt it, like something so nebulous and vast that you could only entertain it for a moment. I have felt it in times when everything was muted, all my emotions at a standstill, numbed for a moment when I could ascend beyond everything and relish in the oneness that is love. It does start with us. We can entertain the notion of loving ourselves as we discover who we are and peel away the layers. We can love ourselves more as we unravel the secret that is our godliness. We are the Creators' light and its love. We feel elation in the instant that we connect to All-That-Is, love permeating our bodies and reality. Beyond that instant, we are dumbfounded at what it has given us, unable to recount or explain the experience at hand. It is honestly an enigma, something beyond words, sound, sight, only attainable through the heart and our connection to the light. We connect with it at Soul Level, all too familiar with this feeling but unable to tell from where. We can only access it by accepting who we are and letting the light from within guide us home. The Creator awaits there and this is our link to it. I suppose some things are not meant to be understood but only appreciated when felt. Ultimately, we are all energy, and this is a reminder that certain abstract notions of the Self can only be revealed on a different plane.

LIVING IN 5D

When you smile, the whole world smiles back at you. The Universe is endless, actually made of multiple parallel universes separated by dimensions of time and space. As infinite and complex as it is, it is also a conscious being that considers us an integral part of it, children of sorts. That being said, it is not passive. It plays a very important role in our lives, actively so. It serves as a mirror for us on an individual and collective basis. What you put out it promptly returns, the same way you did. There has been much talk of instant manifestation in the 5ᵗʰ dimension, of making things appear almost in the blink of an eye by believing they had already happened. This is true on some level, but really much more complex. It always listens, working through a mechanism I will simply call **reciprocity.** We have spent thousands of years within the 3ʳᵈ dimension surviving daily life, completely unaware of the principles of the cosmos. We bathed in our fear, our worries, our anger, and paid the price for these. The 5ᵗʰ dimension calls for the eradication of fear and negativity all together. It is not by principle but by design. It cannot entertain these emotions beyond this point. As we go through life, we send thoughts out all the time. They are as real as something physical, basically vessels for our state of mind at a given moment. Negativity leaves us in an etheric bubble and the Universe accepts that this is our state of mind, returning the favor. It always mirrors who we are. If you look carefully at the world around you in difficult times, you will notice that everything seems to go wrong almost simultaneously. Cynics will call it Murphy's Law. It is in many ways a law, about existing in the NOW. Talking about instant manifestation in somewhat simplified but relevant in that way. Reciprocity means returning the favour.

If someone was in dire need of a car and believed with blind optimism that it would come, without any spiritual understanding, they would almost accept it as if it were already here. This person would be sending very positive signs to the Universe. The Universe would then look at them and see the car as if it already existed. In truth, there would be a gap in the physical world for this car. It would exist in etheric form now, but not in the physical now. This would create a dead space, a **debt** of sorts, that the Universe would have to fill to even out the principle of reciprocity. What is above is below, so it would then come down from thought-form into physicality in some way, and eventually, the optimist would be driving it. The same exact principle goes for negativity. Unfortunately, as we look at world affairs we see there is clearly more fear and anger in the world than positivity. People are entrenched in the adversity of daily life and try to survive by any means necessary. This only propagates the principle of reciprocity for the worse. It can be a gift or a curse. It is true you could have basically anything if you only willed it, but you would have to do it from a clean, positive state of mind. Take a very close look at the people around you that you know are unequivocally happy and optimistic. They do not have to be wealthy or successful by modern standards. They may be totally ascetic. Nonetheless, they are always jubilant and look at the glass as overflowing. It is infectious. They send such positivity all over the place that they never end up needing anything. Their needs are met no matter how minute and simple they may be. The same goes for very negative people that worry all the time, and do not believe they can achieve anything. They will be their own bane, making sure that they do not reach what they set out to. This is all done subconsciously, where foundations are being set. This necessitates for you to believe in the importance of a thought, whether directed towards yourself or others. Every thought counts, they are not fleeting states of mind. All it really is reciprocity. It was never meant to be a punishment, but an amazing gift. In retrospect, we were never meant to live in poverty and war either. Humanity just chose these paths, at least for a large part of the collective consciousness. I will not tell you that things will happen instantly if you decide to change everything tomorrow. You cannot force positivity upon yourself. It is a process you must work on, whereby you eliminate what no longer serves you, release your fears, and evaluate every part of your life, at least those that are harboring fear and anger. It is introspection at its finest. Eventually, provided you take this path and you clear those negative thoughts and emotional baggage, things will come easier to you and you will understand the meaning behind given situations. It is the beginning of a life-changing process. With time you can learn to utilize this gift to your advantage.

It took me a long time to internalize this. My teachers always told me that if I wanted to see my inner state I had only to look at my immediate surroundings. What was inside was outside. I always rationalized that there were other factors at play, other people and dynamics, social, personal, etc…It is a fair argument but the truth is that, in the end, what we send out is what we get, so we can say we attract all these situations to ourselves continuously. We cannot blame society or others for our predicament. Unbelievably, even in the most tumultuous situations we can find solace, but first we must have inner peace. I have reflected long and hard upon my life to this date. I admit that it is me that creates my surroundings through reciprocity. If I leave my house unbalanced, my ego flaring up, angry, bothered, and so on, everything can and will go wrong. The Universe will give me what I put out almost instantly. This is why it is called instant manifestation by many. The point is that as we now enter the 5th dimension, there is no more time for delay. We create now and it comes back to us literally a moment later, therefore it is instant. People that are more attuned and who may have already ascended will feel and understand this as it happens. On a certain day when I have slept and eaten well, and I am feeling positive and relaxed, with my ego in check and in touch with the energy that flows through my heart, I am then happy and secure. Subsequently, the continuum is perfect. Everything falls into place, from catching a taxi during a rainstorm in a crowded area to leaving the house with only 10 dollars in my pocket and managing to do exactly what I set out to. These are the minute details, and it only gets better. I am at peace and I reflect it all around me. People are friendly and amicable, helpful and respectful. They are the stellar opposite when I am upset or unbalanced, even before I look them in the eyes or open my mouth to speak. This is happening faster and faster since the Ascension began. It is said God is in the details. This is true. Look at the moments of your day for clues about yourself and what is bothering you. If everything is going wrong do not get upset. It is a gift. It is telling you what you should reevaluate in your life. It is the way it was meant to go for you. Do not fight it, nor let your ego do the talking for you. There are infinite messages in these situations. Listen and tune in. If you have a very important meeting and everything is going wrong, preventing you from getting there, you get upset. The more upset you get, the worse things become. You are running late, out of time, worries and scenarios are going through your mind. In the continuum of time what will happen has already happened. Some things you cannot fight. So ask "Why?" Does it want to tell you to stop worrying as you come the next day and realize it wasn't a huge deal, and that people are human and understanding? Does it mean to tell you that the job is no longer right for you and you do not want to listen? Does it want to prevent something happening to you? Or does it wish to wake you up to the fact that you are really afraid about your performance and therefore inadvertently delayed your arrival? Only you know the answer. There is no coincidence in this world, so listen to the Universe as it talks to you. The 5th dimension is here. It asks you to understand the principles of its mechanism, your relationship with the Universe, and with yourself. It asks you to change and evolve, to let go of things, regardless of how afraid you may be. Only then can you understand your worth. Times are changing and all they ask is that you change with them. If you refuse and stay set in your ways, the Universe will continue what it does, and you will pay the price instantly. In the end, it is all for the best when you are asked to do some spring cleaning with your emotions. Letting go is difficult, especially in relationships. We can succumb to fear of being alone or of letting go of the security that we feel at the moment. What is it then, really? Is it laziness, fear of turning rocks over and facing the unknown, or is it comfort and dependence? Ask yourself but do not expect an immediate answer. I was in a negative state of mind a while back. It was basically a moment when I was stuck in an archaic behavioural pattern that intervened with my faith. I consider myself to be a very sensible and logical person. I know well enough, after all the things that I have experienced, that I believe, and have faith in who I am. Despite all that, I was still entertaining this negativity and it was mind-boggling to me how I could be so illogical. That night I went out for a walk as I often do when I want solutions. I must have walked a good 4 hours under a full moon, drawing wisdom from the cosmos. I was repeating to myself over and over, out loud: " Why don't I believe?", almost like a madman in search of a fictional, hidden treasure. It didn't make sense to me how I could do this to myself. I kept this going until it hit me like an epiphany, except it was nothing new. I believed in the name of all my experiences, my survival, who I had been and who I had become. I believed unequivocally in myself and my abilities. It was as if I had purged myself of my lack of faith through this process. Sometimes even the most rational people have gaps in logic and must retrace their journey in order to understand something. The point is that I was willing to address how this behavior was no longer befitting the new me, how it was obsolete and had to be dealt with. It was not by some intricate regression session but by asking myself why, and letting the inner voice answer. It took 4 hours, but it answered. It was telling me to change, to let go, to quieten the ego, as it wanted to stay in the past, where there was confusion and doubt. In a state of clarity, it wouldn't feel needed. Too bad. We always change, not just by getting older and wiser, but by lightening the emotional load we carry with us. It demands strength to deal with what we do not want to look into but we are all stronger than we think. It doesn't take extreme circumstances to bring that to the surface.

Achieving a 5th-dimensional state of mind is about truth and introspection. The willingness to listen is imperative. Look at the world of today, more provocative and straightforward than ever, the scandals that arise every day, the clashes between disgruntled youths and dictatorships with archaic, oppressive regimes. Look at the Occupy movement, not only at its political ramifications but at the questions it brings forth about how humanity conducts itself, and how power is allocated; the schemes and manipulations slowly have no place to hide. The 5th dimension does not allow for truth to be hidden. People are awakening all over the globe. Just look at the headlines every day. Yet, the change starts with you, and your awakening. Many YOUs make up humanity, a total of individuals we call the people of Terra. In the end, it is like voting: everyone counts. This new era will leave no stone unturned, it will not allow for anything but light. This will happen in stages, but you will now see the polarity between fear and light. New governments will rise from the rubble of the old ones, and the youth of the world will bring forth new social mores, distant from the opulence and greed of yore.

For now, start with yourself and embrace this New Age, everything will soon be light. Following the storm there is great solace and balance. Start by looking within and embracing the Universe, as you acquiesce to adopting a new attitude. It will reciprocate with love and nurture. It is the greatest gift of all. Consider it a friend, not a foe. Love is light

INDIGO

There is so much to be said about the Indigo generation. It would take a few manuscripts to do so. Some have already been written and they cover the vast notions of the term, therefore there is no need to reiterate anything. This is now a reality and it is upon us. It is part of our everyday life. We witness trying times as a planet as we enter into the New Age. We see uprisings of youths all over the Middle East, Russia, and the United States. The Occupy generation is here. The harsh realities of the world are being addressed directly so that it may face the music and either accept change, or enter a new age of adversity. Most of these movements are led by young people who find no solace or refuge in the modern facets of the world. They realize that there is no future in the way we are living, and that radical changes have to take effect so that we can reclaim our right to live as free citizens of Terra. We all have our God-given rights and yet we see them being violated on a daily basis by the competitive mores of a modern society. The more we progress, the greater the gap between people, and no hope of bridging it. Indigos are here to remedy the situation. They exist beyond the gap, as well as within it. They represent every facet of society, every culture, race, and creed. They come in many forms. Many will lead successful corporate lives despite never finding true fulfillment, while others will pay the price for not being able to adhere to the prerequisites of our society. They will fall into the margins seldom to rise again. They are simply not geared for the reality we live in. They are out-of-the-box thinkers, creative beyond belief, wise beyond their years, but unable to fit into the middle class molds we have created, where everything is pre-set and awaiting. They know inside themselves that their convictions are the right ones but often do not have the faith to follow through and face the adversity that awaits them. Many have taken upon themselves roles of sacrifice, whereby they reflect the ugly faces of our society and all its shunned topics, often by being victims, whether of substance abuse, bullying, or even suicide. We are witnessing in the last 30 years waves of drug use that seem to only get bigger, as people try to find peace within moments of disillusion. As someone who has faced this aspect of life, I thoroughly understand the need for an escape, and it is often too easy to choose this way. The question is from what? Were we to address and honestly reflect upon what we need to change in our value system, the competition, the dog–eat-dog attitude, many things would sort themselves out. This is what they are here to teach us. This will often not be apparent until later, since, to 20th century mindsets the lessons are not direct, but require introspection. Only by reflecting upon this new age can we understand how to cope with change, and not be swallowed by the decay of the obsolete. Gaia has been exploited for personal gain, polluted, forests decimated, rivers poisoned, species annihilated, all in the name of profitability. This has taken on new dimensions since the 1980s, and peaked recently. Population is at an all-time high. Individuals live like modern-day czars while entire populations in Africa, South East Asia, and South America do not even have basic irrigation and food supply. We are now faced with the immense contradiction that the world has become. The media reminds us of this every day, in its own limited way. The internet has found more creative and innovative ways to breach the boundaries of transparency, and show us these hidden facets. Many youths that have gained great success in sports, acting, high technology, and even business, some barely out of high school, have shattered the notion of age and responsibility. The modern world increasingly belongs to them as we witness how public opinion is swayed by bloggers and internet activists.

They basically want to be heard, to be acknowledged, and for the world to understand that what it thinks it knows is only a fraction of the truth. Notions are being gradually shattered and points-of-view altered by this wave. This is the Indigo generation at work. They are all around you. They may be you. I meet so many people on a daily basis, some more obvious than others, that are Indigo Children. They are as young as 12 and as old as in their 60s. They are so different from one another, but, in essence, they are all revolutionaries of the heart. Some are much more polemic than others, while some are content with just awakening those around them. They all share an impatient view of the world, already so aware and with a mind that wants to see what most can only conceive. They are often attention deficit, or have some nervous disorder, as modern psychiatry likes to label things. What they are basically saying is that they are bored and frustrated by archaic systems, from education to corporate frameworks, all the way to their domestic situations. They do not want frameworks at all. Only if they are addressed with the proper respect and legroom, can they thrive, as they are shown by their elders that they are entrusted with their lives and can make the right decisions. Right and wrong have carried us so far. Their validity has expired. They always remind me of the American image of Postwar suburbia where everyone is the same, abiding by the same rules, all in the same framework, and gravely shunning anyone that dare step outside of it. It seems so ludicrous today as all we see in our modern culture is self-expression and the desire for individuality. Most people in their 30s have "baby boomers" as parents. They have an equally difficult time accepting the world of today as their own parents had of the world then. The difference is that, for many years, what we call progress had a steady incline and society was slow to evolve beyond this. What the planet has seen since the 1960s, from the Free Love generation, the Civil Rights movement in the USA, Punk music in Britain, to Feminism, and the LGBT awakening of the last 15 years, has brought with it unprecedented change. This cannot coexist with current mindsets, the corporate ideology, the greed, or the marginalization of minorities and lower classes. The two have been clashing for the last four decades. What we see today is the culmination of all this, as we embrace the New Age.

The world as a whole is now entering the 5th dimension, where the obsolete will wither away or perish. The world has reached such polarity that the population realizes that it must fight back and reclaim its right to exist as Terrans the way they were meant to. There is no more middle ground, false compromise, or hidden truths. All must be disclosed. It is now a matter of sheer survival as we are in a critical stage of human evolution. Evidently, those propagating the obsolete are not keen on changing things. This is why the Indigo Children were brought here. It is clear that we can find hope and solace in the knowledge that spirituality has given us. We know it is a New Age and things are changing for the better. We know that we are entering a new Golden Era of prosperity and love, and that we will experience the 5th dimension for the first time in 25000 years. Yet, we also know that with humanity it requires an extreme situation for people to realize the gravity of it all. It has to be pushed into the corner in order to understand the need to fight back. Times will get more difficult before they get better. It is all ultimately for the best. Change is never easy. In this case, it depends on the willingness to pursue it. This will determine the magnitude of the circumstances to come. At the moment, we need to ignite this change, sometimes with impetus that is unprecedented. In the last few years we have witnessed the rise and fall of Wikileaks, taking upon itself to disclose the nature of political agendas behind what we witness daily as news and information. We have seen the rise of the Free Media, the guerilla counterpart of its mainstream, corporate sibling. More and more information is being released that hasn't been siphoned through the censorship of special interest groups. We witnessed the advancement of extraterrestrial disclosure, as well as pressure to release alternative free-energy solutions. This is all Indigo energy at work, no matter the shape or form it comes in. All of these very physical realities have to change in order for us to live a futuristic, evolved lifestyle, that is impartial towards human beings and encompasses humanity as a single entity. This is where we are going, and you might be surprised to see this even in your lifetime. In parallel, there is a world of spiritual energy that awakens change in all of us, in Gaia, and connects us to the Creator's light. The physical and the etheric are each addressing their own energies as we begin to experience a quantum leap in human consciousness.

It will all look different in a few years. The exact measure of time is irrelevant so as not to await or expect it. We must reflect upon ourselves within our spheres of life, as to what changes we can undertake to bring this new world closer. The Indigo Children already experience this reality and are thus so frustrated with the status quo. Above all, they ask you for one thing: **to listen**. Listen to the truth within you and listen to theirs and what they envision for the world. Do not judge or try to change them. They are the way they are for a reason. They are your children, brothers, friends, grandchildren. Do not ignore their pleas, and do not disregard them as transient mindsets, but listen. They will never fit the molds you want them to. They are here to shatter and replace them. If you do understand why they are what they are, do not cloak this with disregard. They are here to awaken the change within you and to enlighten you with new possibilities. Let them express themselves and become the people they desire to. Listen and learn from this process. There is always more to learn, regardless of age and education. It comes to us in the most unpredictable forms. We need to collectively change. To do so, we do not need to understand each other, only to accept and respect each other's inalienable right to personal truth. The world of today is convinced that there is only one. It is simply a fallacy. We are each a universe to ourselves. Respect us, love us and let us thrive, dream and explore. To be what we are is really all we can and were meant to be. Yet, it all begins with the freedom to start on this journey. Love how you want to be loved.

Epilogue

IT HAS BEEN approximately a month and a half since I penned my first word in what would become this book. I cannot say that I wrote it so much as it poured through me, notions and ideas yearning to be jotted down so as to take physical form. It had been sitting on me like a wave of energy for so long but I kept on putting it off. In truth, I did not really believe that I could have the patience or dedication to make it happen. I was asked to go through with it and entertained the idea, believing it would be a long and arduous prospect. I really had no clue what it meant. I thought of Norman Mailer and Hemingway and wondered how on Earth I could tackle a project on such a scale. I am not a writer in any capacity. It seemed ridiculous. Then, it just happened. Truth is something we can all share as long as we are willing to go all the way. I have seen myself rise out of dire situations against all odds, experiencing a totally new reality on the way. In retrospect, a story from the heart is one always worth telling. We are all human beings, we are all so closely related, and we can experience ourselves through others. We will always find solace in knowing others have gone the longer, more treacherous path, and come out stronger and wiser. In many ways our journeys are all the same. No matter the circumstances, they often offer the same lessons. Whether or not we choose to listen is another thing. The point is that they not go to waste. Who are we if not the things we pick up along the way? We all have our truths, our own viewpoints, but in the end we all search for balance and love. This transcends everything. I wouldn't have let my journey go to waste, hoping it would touch someone somewhere, even for a fleeting moment. I have poured myself out through these words, holding on to them only for an instant until they became part of this truth. I understand them only in retrospect. This journey has allowed me to trace who I am and re-experience everything from a wiser and more aware stance. I saw the continuity of it all, entertaining the idea of a metamorphosis, and understanding how we can all take a step towards change. I realize I am only a vessel for these words, that it all originated somewhere else long ago. I can only say I am proud and fulfilled knowing I had even the slightest opportunity to peer into their wisdom. I have often wondered why life had taken such a sharp turn, and if things should have been easier. Today I can affirm how thankful I am for having become the man I am today. I wrote myself into these pages as they peered back at me, reminding me of the long way home. I am still in disbelief that this is over and the cycle is complete. I can say I know who I am now, my truth and all it has to give me. I accept who I am, all my mistakes and misfortunes and all they have given me. I have learned to love myself and reality in ways I never imagined possible, a total rebirth of the human spirit.

I want to thank my guides for this opportunity and for the love that kept me going, reminding me of the existence of brighter days. I would like to thank my physical guides that manifested along the way through different faces and personalities. I want to thank my soul-sister Shlomit, as well as A, for the valuable tools and life-lessons. I want to thank myself for believing. I want to thank Gaia, Jimmael and Yahweh for their love and support in my times of disbelief. Most of all I want to thank our father and mother, the Creator, for its love, guidance, and everlasting faith in me when I had none in myself. I thank it for having shown me the way home. Finally, I would like to thank the Indigo generation for all that they are, for all the sacrifices, the hardships and tumultuous times they are facing. I am in awe of their strength, their resolve, their creativity and their appreciation for life. I hope the world never stops asking questions and being surprised by what answers they may yield. I pray that they never stop dreaming so that they share those visions with us some day. I know times will change and light will come, that we will rise to the occasion as we have done before, and that we will mesh into a single face we call human, effacing ideals of gender, race, creed, and archaic dogma, from our home planet. I know this day is coming. Until then, I am proud to be here to see this happening.

Made in the USA
Coppell, TX
01 March 2021